Beyond Debt

A Blueprint To Financial Freedom

Victor Stroia

Copyright © 2023 by Victor Stroia

All rights reserved.

No portion of this book may be reproduced in any form without written permission from the publisher or author, except for brief quotations embodied in critical reviews or otherwise permitted by copyright law.

This book is intended to provide general information regarding personal finance and debt management. The author and publisher have made every effort to ensure the accuracy and completeness of the information contained within. However, neither the author nor the publisher can guarantee that the reader will achieve specific financial outcomes or results by following the advice and strategies discussed in this book. The information provided in this book is not intended to replace or serve as a substitute for any professional or expert financial advice. It is always recommended to consult with a financial advisor, accountant, or other qualified financial professionals before making any significant decisions regarding your personal finances.

Book Cover by: Vivienne Brown

Layout by: Ingrid Olsen

ISBN: 9798860144682

2023

Contents

Introduction		1
1.	Mindset shift	5
2.	The Debt Psychology	23
3.	Good Debt vs. Bad Debt	35
4.	Credit Scores	51
5.	The Battle Plan	74
6.	Assess Your Financial Situation	85
7.	Create a budget	104
8.	Increase Your Income	122
9.	Reduce Expenses	138
10.	Don't Go Overboard	148
11.	Debt Snowball vs. Debt Avalanche	159
12.	Debt Consolidation & Refinancing Options	172
13.	Dealing with Debt Collectors	186
14.	Build an Emergency Fund	200

15. Stay Motivated and Persistent	209
16. Going Beyond	225
Conclusion	240

Introduction

Hey there! I know you bought this book because you're eager to tackle your debt and regain control over your finances. You're not alone, and I'm here to help you break free from the chains of debt and embrace a life of financial freedom and success.

I know first-hand the impact that excessive debt can have on your life. I've been there myself when I was in my mid-30s. And as much as I'd like to tell you I was fighting with it, the truth is I wasn't fighting; I was drowning in debt and most of it was in maxed-out credit cards. I was paying so much in interest that I could barely keep up with the minimum payments. I felt like I was in a never-ending cycle of debt, and it was taking a toll on my mental health and overall well-being.

It took a major setback that served as a kick in the backside to finally, wake me up to the hole I dug myself into. I made a commitment to myself, then, to get out of debt and take control of my finances. It wasn't easy, and it wasn't fun, but with hard work and determination, I was able to pay off my debt and start building wealth for myself and my family.

So, what's my secret weapon to help you conquer your debt? I'm going to teach you how to harness the power of a winner's mindset. This mindset is all about dreaming big, setting goals, and taking action to achieve them. It's a game-changer! With a winner's mindset in your arsenal, you'll be unstoppable in your quest for financial freedom.

Throughout this book, I'll cover every aspect of what it takes to become debt-free and financially savvy. We'll begin by evaluating your current financial situation to understand where you stand and identify any areas that need improvement. I'll show you how to create a budget that works for you, one that's realistic, effective, and makes it easy to track your progress.

Next up, we'll explore a multitude of ways to increase your income. We'll discuss side hustles, negotiating pay raises, investing, and more. With determination and creativity, you'll be able to boost your income and accelerate your debt repayment journey.

I'll also share with you the ins and outs of effective debt repayment strategies. We'll talk about the debt snowball and avalanche methods, consolidation, and more. It's essential to understand the psychological aspects of debt, so we'll explore that too, as well as the difference between good and bad debt. By the end of our journey, you'll be armed with knowledge and ready to rise above your financial challenges.

Along the way, I'll share stories of real people who have successfully conquered their debt using a winner's mindset, as well as practical tips and advice to keep you motivated and on track. I'll also provide helpful tools and resources, such as debt repayment calculators, budgeting templates, and more.

Now, this is important; I want you to believe in yourself and your ability to conquer your debt. Your determination to succeed, your willingness to overcome obstacles and your commitment to change will form the bedrock of your journey. It may seem daunting right now, but once you start applying the right techniques to your financial life, you'll be amazed at what you can achieve. So, embrace the challenge and have faith in yourself!

This journey will be challenging. I'm going to be brutally honest, I won't sugar-coat anything and I'll call things for what they are. If you're expecting a cuddle and a pat on the back, you took the wrong pill. I promise though, it will also be incredibly rewarding, and you'll come out on the other side with newfound confidence and financial know-how.

I'm going to push you to take action because I want you to get out of debt and achieve the success you deserve. Remember, this journey is all about having the right mindset, tools, and determination. With my guidance and your commitment, you'll soon be celebrating your debt-free life and enjoying the rewards of your hard work.

Think of the taste of victory, of looking at your balance sheet and seeing zero debt, of the financial independence that allows you to make choices on your terms. This is the reward awaiting you at the end of this challenging journey. I am here to accompany you, to guide you, and to celebrate with you when you finally break those chains of debt and begin to enjoy the fruits of your hard work. You have it within you to overcome your financial challenges, and together, we will get there.

So, are you ready to make some magic happen? Let's dive in and start turning your financial dreams into reality. Together, we'll conquer your debt and unlock the door to a prosperous, fulfilling, and financially secure future!

Chapter 1

Mindset shift

Ah, now we're getting to the heart of the matter. This is where the real transformation begins, where we start to peel back the layers and get to the core of your financial journey. You see, getting out of debt isn't just about crunching numbers, making payments, and ticking boxes. Sure, those things are important, and we'll definitely cover them later in the book. But before we dive into the nitty-gritty, you need to adopt a winner's mindset, a mindset that will be your rocket fuel, propelling you towards your worthy goals and dreams.

You need to build up an excitement and hunger for success and financial freedom that's so intense it's almost palpable. You need to be so fired up, so ready for change that you can practically taste the freedom that comes with being debt-free. This isn't just about wanting to get out of debt, it's about needing to, it's about not being able to stand the thought of another day, another minute, in the chains of financial burden.

And it's also about the vision. You need to visualise yourself not just achieving your end goal, but also overshooting and exceeding it. You need to see yourself not just reaching the finish line, but sprinting past it, leaving your old financial troubles in the dust. This is about more than just getting by; it's about thriving and building a life of abundance and financial security.

In this chapter, we'll delve into the importance of mindset and how to cultivate the right attitude to conquer your debt and achieve financial freedom. We'll explore how to harness the power of positive thinking, how to set ambitious yet achievable goals, and how to stay motivated even when the going gets tough. We'll look at how to turn setbacks into comebacks, and how to use your past financial mistakes as stepping stones to a brighter, debt-free future.

So buckle up, because we're about to embark on a transformative journey that will change not just your financial situation, but your entire life.

The Power of a Winner's Mindset

A winner's mindset is all about believing in yourself, setting ambitious goals, and taking action to achieve them. It's about refusing to settle for mediocrity and pushing yourself to reach your full potential. When you adopt a winner's mindset, you become unstoppable in your quest for success.

BEYOND DEBT

Let me tell you a story. I interviewed a number of people who had gotten out of debt while I was doing the research for this book. One of them, let's call him Bob, was knee-deep in debt, and he couldn't see a way out. All he did was play the victim, feeling sorry for himself and binge-watching rubbish on TV.

The problem was that none of these seemed to help with his ever-growing debt. He had about £13000 worth of debt in credit cards alone, all maxed out of course, plus a few other loans. It all went well for a while as he was able to meet the minimum payments every month. But as his expenses rose and his pay failed to keep pace, he started dipping back into the credit cards almost as soon as he was paying them.

The light bulb moment came when, one month after having lost track of loan repayments, credit cards, utilities and some other expenses, he forgot about the rent and didn't have any more money to cover it. That really got him scared and opened his eyes to the hole he'd dug himself into. He realised he just couldn't keep going like this and had to do something about his debt. It wasn't even an option as the problem was getting worse by the month. It was a do-or-die kind of thing. So he looked online, educated himself, asked for advice, made a plan and took action.

Only 12 months later, he was almost completely out of debt and had a fleet of mobile healthy fast-food outlets that he sends to fairs and events all around the country generating income for him.

Look, you don't even need this book to tell you how to pay off your debt; the information is everywhere. Everybody knows that in order to escape debt you have to spend less and earn more, but very few people are doing it. And that's because they are not committed and don't have that winner's mindset. They wish for things to happen, instead of making things happen. "People need to replace their wishbone with a backbone," I heard someone say once.

Here's the bottom line: your mindset is the bedrock of your financial journey. If you don't believe in yourself and your ability to overcome debt, you'll struggle to make headway. But when you embrace a winner's mindset, just like Bob did, you'll find the motivation and determination to tackle your debt head-on and achieve your financial goals. Remember, Bob didn't just wish for his debt to disappear; he made it happen. And with a winner's mindset, you can do the same.

How to Cultivate a Winner's Mindset

So, how do you develop a winner's mindset? Here are some key steps to get you started.

Set clear, ambitious goals:

Define your financial goals and be specific about what you want to achieve. You can't hit a target if you don't know what it is.

And you can't reach your goals if you're not clear on what they are. When your goals are vague, it's easy to get lost. Imagine you're a ship setting sail without a clear destination. You're likely to end up drifting aimlessly, not making much progress and possibly even ending up somewhere you don't want to be. The same is true in life. If your goal is something like "I want to be successful," or "I want to make a lot of money," where do you even start with that? How do you know when you've achieved it? How do you define success? What does "a lot of money" actually mean to you? Most people don't set clear goals because they are afraid they'll be disappointed in case they don't achieve them. So their first thought is negative "Oh, I'm not gonna achieve it". Even worse, if they tell someone about it they may end up disappointed and ridiculed. But this is wrong. This fear of disappointment and ridicule can keep you from trying anything in your life and guess how you'll end up at 80? Disappointed and ridiculed; not for having failed, but for not having tried. That is failure by default.

So go on and set clear and ambitious goals knowing that you can change them anytime you see fit and it's nobody's business why you did so. When your goals are clear and specific, you have a destination in mind. You know exactly what you're aiming for. You can develop a plan, a roadmap to get you there. You can measure your progress, adjust your course as needed, and stay focused and motivated because you know exactly what you're working towards.

Now you have a target to aim for, and you can start breaking that goal down into smaller, achievable steps. You can start developing a plan to get you there, and every decision you make can be guided by that goal.

So take the time to get really clear on what you want. Make your goals specific, measurable, achievable, relevant, and time-bound - or what's often called SMART. This way, you're not just dreaming, you're planning for success, and that will keep you focused and motivated.

Believe in yourself:

Trust in your ability to overcome debt and achieve financial freedom. Remember, you are capable of greatness, and you deserve success. If you don't believe in yourself, who will? Without a strong belief in yourself, you'll crumble at the first sign of resistance.

Look, I get it. Self-doubt creeps in. We all have those moments when we wonder if we're good enough, smart enough, talented enough, or anything enough. But you've got to fight that. You've got to push back against those doubts and remind yourself of your worth, your potential, and your power. People have a tendency to doubt their beliefs and believe their doubts.

Believing in yourself isn't about being arrogant or thinking you're the dog's bollocks; it's about knowing, deep down, that you are capable. It's about trusting in your abilities, your talents, your drive, and your determination.

You've got to believe in yourself before anyone else will. The world around you will do a good enough job of beating you down and discouraging you. Don't be one of them. Talk yourself up and know you'll succeed. Don't hope, don't wish, and don't pray to succeed; KNOW you'll succeed. Confidence is contagious. When you believe in yourself, others will believe in you too.

Be bold:

Think big and aim high. Don't settle for small, incremental improvements like just paying off your debt. Strive for massive, life-changing results like paying off your debt and starting a side hustle that will ensure you'll never be forced back into debt. Set goals that are going to force you to stretch, to grow, to become more, better, and faster than you are right now. Have goals that are going to demand your full commitment, your full energy, and your full potential.

This is how you generate momentum behind your initial growth phase and you'll find yourself, not just paying off your debt, but overshooting that target by miles and end up creating wealth for yourself and your family.

You'll hear a lot of people say the secret to success is setting small goals and achieving them. I'm going to call bullshit on that. The secret to success is setting big hairy goals and then exceeding them. There is no great achiever in the world that got there by setting small goals. If you dream small you will end up smaller. Start with the big dream and then divide that into smaller steps and create a plan to get you there. And if you only get halfway you'll still be better off than reaching a small and insignificant goal that doesn't fulfil or make you proud. If it's worth doing, it's worth doing big.

Take action:

Don't just dream about success; take action to make it happen. Be relentless in your pursuit of your goals and never give up. Waiting for the right time is an excuse for laziness. How can you identify the right time for action when you don't know the future? Steve Jobs said, "You can only connect the dots backwards". You don't know whether tomorrow will bring a better opportunity or not. The right time is today, NOW! Not next week, not tomorrow, not after this episode of whatever sticky soapy rubbish you've been binge-watching since the last ice age.

Let me give you another story here. One other guy I've interviewed for this book is a doctor in a hospital and he told me: "Vick, I got to a point where I was feeling physically ill. I was having panic attacks with shortness of breath and racing heart rate which made me unable sometimes to care for my patients.

Then I realised this could put me in danger of losing my job which made it even worse. I even took on new debt to cover the old debt, and that made the hole even bigger but I didn't know what else to do. I was going down a spiral and I knew it but I couldn't see a way out. That's when I decided to take action because I could see the bottom I was heading towards and it didn't look pretty. I called in sick for a few days, claiming I had a chest infection, so I could clear my head and weigh my options. I sat down with a pen and a piece of paper and tried to assess my financial situation. And that's when it hit me; I didn't even know how much I owed, to whom or how much interest I was paying. Of course, I had a vague idea but it was all blurry and unclear because I was even afraid to look. That was both scary and exciting. Scary because I realised I was capable of such an error but also exciting because I saw there were things I could do to stop my money bleeding away."

Now, the interview is quite extensive but at the time of writing, this doctor has paid off all of his debt and started a side hustle in which he also involved his wife and one of their three children. It turns out that his wife didn't even know the level of debt he was in or the depth of his despair and she was already thinking about divorce because his behaviour was becoming unbearable. Unfortunately, this seems to be a common theme among those I interviewed.

Don't let this happen to you. This guy was lucky, he took action just in time to save his financial future, his family and, who knows, maybe even his life. In the end, it worked out well for him, but it almost didn't.

You don't have to wait until you're on the edge of the cliff to finally do the right thing. You don't have to reach the bottom of the downward spiral to wake up. Take action now, before you damage yourself and those you love and care for. "I'll do it tomorrow" is a lie you'll tell yourself tomorrow the same way you did today and so on until another tomorrow. How many tomorrows can you stand? How many tomorrows before it's too late and there's no tomorrow?

Start moving towards your financial freedom small step by small step and you will soon start building momentum that will carry you to your end goal and beyond. The further you go the easier it gets but you'll have to get the wagon moving first. Remember, results will never come before you take action. You can dream about success until the cows come home but if you don't do something about it you'll grow roots in your sofa waiting for it and it will never happen for you.

Learn from failure:

So, now we get to talk about failure, or Santa Claus, or the Tooth Fairy. Am I losing the plot? Well, maybe not just yet. Please stay with me here because I think this is really important.

So, what do you think these three concepts have in common? Can you guess? Here's the answer and please don't forget this:

None of them is real unless we accept them as such. They don't exist until we actualize them with our acceptance. Take a five-year-old child for example. To him, both Santa and the Tooth Fairy are very real. Now, if you're going to try to convince your five-year-old child that Santa doesn't exist, you should, probably, take your luggage to your psychiatric therapist, 'cause you're going to be there a while.

What that child doesn't believe in, however, is failure. It's just not real for him and therefore he will pursue his goal with relentless action and commitment until either he achieves it himself or you, one step away from a nervous meltdown, decide to give him whatever he bloody wants. That, of course, will reinforce his belief that he can attain any goal he sets his mind on, therefore keeping the concept of failure out of his awareness. Which is how it should be for any child by the way.

Don't you think you would achieve more if you showed the same passion and commitment towards your goals and dreams? Of course, you would. You would move mountains if you didn't accept failure. I've heard people say "Failure is not an option". That's a load of bullshit. What's that supposed to mean anyway? If is not an option, then it's a given right? And you don't have any control over it, right? Look what this does to your mind. Of course, failure is an option, and it's down to you not to choose that option. Take control! "Oh, but what if I take control and flop?" I hear you ask. So what? See what went wrong, adjust, and try again. And again, and again, and again until you succeed because you don't know any other way. You don't know what failure means. You don't have that concept; it's just a meaningless word to you. Have you ever heard the saying, "I succeeded because I didn't know I couldn't"? Well, now you know what it means.

Look, failure is not failure until you accept it as such. Otherwise, it is just a setback, a hurdle to overcome, and a chance to learn, to grow, and to better yourself. The moment you accept failure, you make a choice to quit, to give up, and to throw away all the progress you have made so far. You will ditch all the effort, the sweat, the blood, the tears and the dedication you have invested in whatever you're now giving up. And you know what the funny thing is? Tomorrow you will have to start something else, FROM GROUND ZERO!

Napoleon Hill said, "The ladder of success is never crowded at the top". Do you know why that is? It's because most people give up along the way and usually just before they would have hit paydirt. And then they start something else and give up and start something else and give up, and then they die; unfulfilled, unloved, bitter and grumpy. They always end up spending more energy, time, and effort achieving virtually nothing, than the one who sticks his teeth into a big juicy goal and doesn't let go until he feels that sweet taste of victory. What exactly do you think you're accomplishing by giving up? Who do you think you're fooling when you quit? Life is not going to give you a break; it will be there tomorrow morning to confront you.

So GET UP! Dust yourself off, adjust your plan, and KEEP GOING! You may be only a few steps away from your success story.

Surround yourself with positive influences:

That is a nice way of saying: get rid of negative people around you. You don't need any griping and eternally complaining boneheads around to tell you how hard it will be and how you'll never make it. There must be no room for negativity in your world. You've got to cut loose the anchors of pessimism, the naysayers, the doubters, the ones who tell you it's impossible. Those people are like quicksand, pulling you down into their pit of mediocrity faster than you can say "debt-free."

Instead, you need to be rubbing shoulders with the movers and shakers, the dreamers and doers, the ones who've tasted success and are hungry for more. These are the people who will fuel your ambition, ignite your drive, and push you to reach for the stars. They're the ones who've walked the path, weathered the storms, and come out on top. Learn from their triumphs, their setbacks, and their resilience. Let their stories inspire you, their wisdom guide you, and their energy propel you forward.

And it's not just about taking, it's about giving back too. Share your own journey, your own lessons, and your own victories. Be a beacon of positivity, a source of inspiration, a force of motivation.

You are the sum of the five people you surround yourself with most. So, who's it going to be? The negative Nancys and Debbie Downers who've never done a damn thing with their lives? Or the real success stories, the ones who've actually achieved something, and made a difference? It's your call.

Remember, you're the boss of your life. You get to decide who gets a seat at your table. So choose wisely, because your financial freedom, your future, and your legacy are on the line.

Invest in personal development:

You've got to be on a relentless pursuit of self-improvement. This means diving headfirst into education, training, books, podcasts, and deep self-reflection. Books aren't a luxury, they're a necessity. Ignorance is the real expense here. All the big players, the real achievers, they've got personal libraries that would put some public ones to shame. They're constantly attending seminars, enrolling in courses, always learning, and always growing. And if you think they do this because they've got money to burn, you've got it all backwards. The books, the courses, the seminars, they're the reason they're rolling in dough, not the other way around.

Look, I'm not saying you need to go out and buy a hundred books from the get-go. Start with one. The average bloke in the Western world reads one book a year, and that's usually some fiction fluff. If you make it your mission to read and truly absorb one book a week, you'll have an advantage of more than 50-1 compared to the average Joe. And if you're one of those "I don't have time to read" types, get them in audio format and listen to them on your way to and from work, at the gym, whilst you're cooking dinner. Turn every scrap of dead time into a learning session to help you grow.

The more you grow, the more capable you'll become in slaying your debt and achieving financial freedom. You're not just reading a book; you're investing in your future. You're not just listening to a podcast; you're building your empire. You're not just attending a seminar; you're paving your road to success.

The key to wealth isn't just making money, it's making yourself. So invest in you, because you're the best asset you've got.

The Impact of a Winner's Mindset on Your Debt Journey

When you adopt a winner's mindset, it's like flipping a switch in your brain. Suddenly, your entire approach to debt repayment transforms. You become more focused, more determined, and more resilient in the face of challenges. You're not just some bloke trying to pay off his debts; you're a champion in the ring, ready to knock out your debt for good.

With a winner's mindset, you're not just willing to take risks, you're eager to. You're ready to explore new strategies, to think outside the box, to accelerate your debt repayment. You're not just playing the game, you're changing the game.

And let's not forget about commitment. Your financial goals aren't just something you're working towards; they're something you're committed to. Even when the going gets tough, even when you're faced with setbacks, you're not going to throw in the towel. You're not going to fall back into old habits or give up. You're going to dig your heels in, grit your teeth, and keep pushing forward.

In short, a winner's mindset isn't just a key to unlocking your full potential, it's the master key. It's the key to achieving the financial freedom you've always dreamed of. It's the key to living a life free from the shackles of debt. So, embrace this mindset, let it guide you, let it drive you. Let it be your north star on your journey to a debt-free life.

You're not just paying off debt, you're building a future. You're not just saving money, you're creating wealth. You're not just surviving, you're thriving. So adopt that winner's mindset, and let it guide you on your journey to a debt-free life.

Summary and Key Takeaways

As we conclude this chapter, it's important to reflect on the transformative power of a winner's mindset. This isn't a mere concept or a fleeting thought; it's a profound shift in your approach to life and finances. It's about seeing beyond the immediate challenges of debt and envisioning a future of financial freedom and abundance. It's about believing in your ability to make that vision a reality, no matter how daunting the journey may seem.

The stories we've shared in this chapter, like Bob's, are not just tales of financial turnaround; they are testimonies to the power of a winner's mindset. They are proof that when you believe in yourself, set clear goals, take decisive action, learn from setbacks, surround yourself with positivity, invest in personal growth, and remain committed to your journey, you can overcome even the most overwhelming debt and build a life of financial security and prosperity.

The journey to financial freedom isn't a sprint; it's a marathon. It's not about quick fixes or overnight success; it's about consistent effort, unwavering determination, and relentless pursuit of your goals. It's about adopting a winner's mindset and letting it fuel your journey every step of the way.

So, as we close this chapter, I invite you to take a moment to reflect on your own mindset. Are you ready to adopt a winner's mindset? Are you ready to take control of your financial future? Are you ready to embark on a journey that will not only transform your finances but your entire life?

If your answer is yes, then buckle up. You're about to embark on an exciting journey towards financial freedom. And remember, this journey isn't just about reaching your destination; it's about who you become along the way. So embrace the journey, adopt a winner's mindset, and let's start building your debt-free future.

Chapter 2

The Debt Psychology

Now that we dealt with the mindset shift, let's have a look at the emotional and psychological aspects of debt. We're not just talking about numbers and interest rates here, oh no! We're going deep into the very heart of the matter, the human side of debt. We're going to unravel the tangled web of emotions, behaviours, and decisions that debt can weave around our lives.

You see, debt isn't just a financial issue; it's a deeply personal one too and it can affect your mood, your relationships, and even your health. It's a heavy chain that can weigh you down, making every step feel like a struggle.

You need to be aware of the triggers that can lead you into the debt trap, buying things you don't actually need, and often, don't even really want. Most people, myself included until not so long ago, tend to bury their heads in the sand, ignoring the problem until it's grown into a monstrous debt mountain.

So let's find some solutions and techniques to overcome these psychological pitfalls, shall we?

The Emotional Impact of Debt

Debt is not just a financial burden; it's an emotional one too. The constant worry about making ends meet, the stress of juggling multiple payments, and the fear of what might happen if you can't pay can lead to anxiety, depression, and even physical health problems. It can strain relationships, lower self-esteem, and diminish overall quality of life.

Much more than a financial issue, like numbers on a screen or bills on your doormat, debt is an emotional state. It's the knot in your stomach when you hear the post box, the stress that keeps you up at night, the anxiety that gnaws at you all day, and the shame that makes you want to hide away from the world.

When you're in debt, it feels like you're carrying the weight of the world on your shoulders, dragging you down, and making every step a struggle. It's exhausting, it's demoralising, and it's all-consuming.

I'm not talking from books here. I've been there myself. I've walked down that path of despair, where every step felt like a stumble, every breath a struggle. I was sinking, drowning in a sea of failure. The weight of the world seemed to be on my shoulders, and I was buckling under the pressure. I was unable to fulfil the basic role of a provider for my family, unable to ensure their comfort and security.

The guilt was suffocating. It was as if I was trapped in a room with no doors, no windows, just four walls closing in on me. I felt like I was failing those who depended on me, those who believed in me. The guilt wasn't just about not being able to provide materially, it was about not being able to provide emotionally, not being able to be the pillar of strength my family needed.

And then there was the feeling of uselessness. It was as if I was a cog in a machine that had stopped turning, a part that had become redundant. I felt like I was standing on the sidelines, watching life pass me by, unable to participate, unable to contribute. It was a feeling of being disconnected, of being irrelevant.

These feelings were not just overwhelming, they were all-consuming. They seeped into every aspect of my life, tainting every moment with a sense of despair and hopelessness. But I share this not to dwell on the past, but to let you know that I understand. I've been there, I've felt that pain, and I've come out the other side. And if I can do it, so can you.

And here's the thing: you're not alone. Millions of people are in the same boat, battling the same emotions, facing the same challenges. And just like them, you have the strength and the resilience to overcome this. You have the power to turn your situation around, to lift that weight off your shoulders, and to break free. It won't be easy, and it won't happen overnight, but with determination, perseverance, and a little bit of help, you can do it.

Debt can make you feel ashamed. You might feel like you've failed, like you're not good enough. But let me tell you something: you're not a failure. You're just someone who's hit a bump in the road. And bumps in the road are there to make us slow down, reassess our direction, and find a better path forward.

So, let's do just that. Let's slow down, let's reassess, and let's find a better path forward. Let's explore the emotional impact of debt, let's understand it, let's face it, and let's overcome it.

Why Do We End Up In Debt?

So, what leads us into debt in the first place? Often, it's psychological triggers that push us to spend beyond our means. The desire for instant gratification, the pressure to keep up with societal standards, and the temporary relief from stress or sadness that retail therapy provides, all contribute to unnecessary spending and debt accumulation.

We all do it and I'm guilty of that too. About a year ago a good friend of mine asked me to visit him at his recording studio and maybe put a song together. I haven't seen my friend in years and couldn't resist the temptation so I picked up my guitar and off I went. Five hours went like ten minutes and we had a great time.

We caught up, played silly old songs, had a laugh, but in the end came up with a pretty good song and it sounded great on his equipment.

Now, I'm a sucker for sound equipment and especially power amplifiers. I used to build them from scratch when I was young and sell them to night clubs and party venues. So about two days after visiting my friend at the studio, I found myself, not just shopping for, but actually buying a 250W, studio quality, all singing and dancing, sound system. To this day that system has never been used at anything more than 10% of its capacity. Also worth mentioning, my two kids were aged 1 and 4 at the time of the purchase, so I knew I had no chance of hearing its full power.

So why did I buy a 250W sound system when I could have spent less than a third on a 50W system with the same results? Well, it was a well-known brand that just happened to advertise quite aggressively on telly at the time and it was the same brand my friend was using as monitors in his studio.

So I fell victim to almost all of the triggers. I felt I can reward myself for having done well with the song, so that's instant gratification. I wanted to keep up with my friend in terms of equipment, although I had no need for so much output power. And if there was any glimmer of hope that I'll stop myself in time, it got blown away by the TV advertising.

Marketers are well aware of these triggers and design strategies to exploit them. They create a sense of urgency with limited-time offers, appeal to our desire for status with luxury brands, and offer easy credit options that make big purchases seem more affordable.

Rationalization and the Illusion of Control

The story of my 250W sound system purchase is a classic example of how we rationalize our unnecessary spending. I convinced myself that I needed this high-powered system, even though I knew I would never use it to its full capacity. I justified the purchase by telling myself that I deserved it for creating a great song, that it was a symbol of my success, and that it was a necessary tool for my hobby. This is a common psychological trap that many of us fall into. We convince ourselves that we need something, and then we find reasons to justify the purchase.

Another psychological factor at play here is the illusion of control. We like to believe that we are in control of our decisions and that we are immune to the influences of marketing and societal pressures. But the reality is, we are often swayed by these external factors without even realizing it. The aggressive advertising, the brand reputation, and the desire to match my friend's equipment all influenced my decision to buy the sound system. I thought I was making an independent, rational decision, but in reality, I was being manipulated by these external factors.

Understanding these psychological triggers is the first step towards better financial management. We need to be aware of our tendencies to rationalize unnecessary spending and to fall for the illusion of control. We need to question our motives and examine whether our desires are genuine or influenced by external factors.

The next time you find yourself about to make a big purchase, take a step back and ask yourself: Do I really need this? Is this a rational decision or am I trying to justify unnecessary spending? Am I in control of this decision or am I being influenced by external factors?

By asking these questions, we can start to break the cycle of unnecessary spending and debt accumulation. We can start to make more informed, rational decisions that align with our financial goals and values. And most importantly, we can start to take control of our financial future.

The Boiling Frog Principle and Debt

Ever heard of the boiling frog principle? It's a metaphor that packs a punch, a tale that's been told time and again to illustrate how we humans can be blissfully unaware of gradual changes until we're in hot water; literally.

Here's the idea: if you were to drop a frog into a pot of boiling water, it would leap out immediately, instinctively recognising the danger. But if you were to place that same frog in a pot of lukewarm water and then slowly, oh so slowly, turn up the heat, that frog would stay put. It would swim around, oblivious, as the water gradually heated up. And by the time it realised what was happening, it would be too late to jump out. Grim, isn't it?

Now, before you get your knickers in a twist, let me assure you: no frogs have been harmed in the writing of this book. It's a fable, a cautionary tale. But it's one that holds a powerful lesson, especially when it comes to the slippery slope of debt.

You see, debt is a sneaky beast. It doesn't pounce; it creeps. It's not a tsunami that knocks you off your feet; it's a rising tide that slowly but surely engulfs you. One day, it's a credit card bill that's a smidge higher than you'd like. The next, it's a loan you had to take out for an unexpected expense. Bit by bit, pound by pound, the debt piles up. And before you know it, you're in over your head, drowning in a sea of red that you didn't even see coming.

That, my friends, is the boiling frog principle in action. Just like our froggy friend in the slowly heated pot, we fail to recognise the danger until we're well and truly cooked. We ignore the warning signs, we brush off the rising heat, and we end up in a financial pickle that's hotter and more dangerous than anything we could have imagined.

But there is hope. Have a look in the mirror; do you look like a frog? If you do, give yourself a kiss; you might be a prince. But chances are you don't, so unlike the frog, you can change your situation. You can spot the warning signs, you can take action, and you can leap out of that pot. It's not a walk in the park, mind you. It takes guts, grit, and a good deal of determination. But it's absolutely doable. And the first and most important step is to notice the pot around you and the water warming up.

Overcoming Psychological Weaknesses

The first step in overcoming our psychological weaknesses is awareness. We need to recognize our triggers, understand our emotional responses, and acknowledge our rationalizations. We need to be brutally honest with ourselves about our spending habits and our attitudes towards money. This isn't about blaming or shaming ourselves; it's about understanding and accepting our current situation so that we can start making positive changes.

Once we've gained this awareness, we can start to challenge our unhealthy beliefs and behaviours. We can question our need for instant gratification, resist the pressure to keep up with societal standards, and find healthier ways to cope with stress and sadness. We can challenge our rationalizations and confront our illusion of control. We can start to make more informed, rational decisions that align with our financial goals and values.

One effective technique for challenging these psychological weaknesses is cognitive restructuring. This is a type of cognitive-behavioural therapy that involves identifying and challenging irrational or negative thoughts. For example, if you find yourself thinking, "I deserve this expensive purchase because I've had a hard week," you can challenge this thought by asking yourself, "Is this purchase really going to make me feel better in the long run? Is there a less expensive way I can reward myself? Is this purchase in line with my financial goals?"

Another technique is mindfulness. This involves paying attention to the present moment without judgment. When you find yourself about to make an impulsive purchase, take a moment to pause and observe your thoughts and feelings. Notice the desire for instant gratification, the pressure to conform, the urge to escape from stress or sadness. Acknowledge these feelings without judgment, and then make a conscious decision to act in a way that aligns with your financial goals.

Finally, don't underestimate the power of support. Whether it's a financial advisor, a trusted friend, or a support group, having someone to talk to can make a huge difference. They can provide objective feedback, offer encouragement, and help you stay accountable to your financial goals.

Overcoming psychological weaknesses is not an overnight process. It takes time, patience, and perseverance. But with each small victory, you'll gain confidence and momentum. And before you know it, you'll be on your way to financial freedom.

Remember, you're not a frog. You're a human being with the power to change your situation. You have the ability to recognize the rising heat, to leap out of the pot, and to create a better financial future for yourself. So take a deep breath, roll up your sleeves, and let's get to work. Because you're not just overcoming debt; you're building a life of financial freedom and peace of mind. And that, my friends, is worth every bit of effort.

Summary and Key Takeaways

Understanding the psychology behind debt is a monumental step in your journey towards financial freedom. It's like turning on a light in a dark room. Suddenly, you can see the obstacles in your path, the traps that have been holding you back. You can see the patterns of behaviour that have led you into debt, and you can start to change them.

But let's be clear: this isn't a walk in the park. It's a climb up a mountain. It's challenging, it's tough, and there will be times when you'll want to give up. But remember, the view from the top is worth it. The sense of accomplishment, the freedom, the peace of mind - it's all waiting for you at the top.

And here's the thing: you're not climbing this mountain alone. Millions of people are on the same journey, battling the same obstacles, facing the same challenges. You're part of a community, a brotherhood and sisterhood of warriors fighting for financial freedom. And just like them, you have the strength and the resilience to reach the summit.

You have the power to turn your situation around, to lift the weight of debt off your shoulders, and to break free from the chains that have been holding you back. It won't be easy, and it won't happen overnight, but with determination, perseverance, and a little bit of help, you can do it.

So, let's take a moment to celebrate how far you've come. You've acknowledged the problem, you've faced the reality of your situation, and you've taken the first steps towards change. That's huge. That's progress. And it's something to be proud of.

In the next chapter, we're going to roll up our sleeves and get down to business. We're going to delve into practical steps you can take to start tackling your debt. We're going to talk about strategies, techniques, and tools you can use to pay off your debt and build a brighter financial future.

Remember, you're not alone in this journey. With each step, you're moving closer to a debt-free life. With each victory, no matter how small, you're proving to yourself and the world that you're stronger than your debt, that you're not defined by your financial past, and that you have the power to shape your financial future.

So, let's keep going. Let's keep climbing. Let's keep fighting for that view from the top. Because I promise you, it's worth it.

Chapter 3

Good Debt vs. Bad Debt

Now, let's take a wild ride down the lanes of good and bad debt. This isn't your grandma's finance book. It's more like that brutally honest, wise-cracking uncle who drops truth bombs with a wink and a nod. And before you roll your eyes, no, Good Debt isn't debt you've swindled away under your mattress, away from prying eyes.

To make it easier to understand, let's use a bit of an unconventional approach. We're going to deconstruct and redefine them using an idea that's as basic as it is significant: assets and liabilities. Now, I can practically hear the outraged squawks of financial analysts who love their complex terminologies and definitions. To them, this might appear too simplistic or even borderline heretical, but bear with me.

When you strip away all the unnecessary jargon, an asset is fundamentally something that puts money into your pocket. It could be a business, a real estate property, an investment, or anything that generates income. Conversely, a liability takes money out of your pocket. It's the credit card bill, the car loan, the expensive designer shoe addiction, basically anything that causes your hard-earned money to fly away.

With this in mind, let's go back to our main characters. Good debt is the debt you take on to invest in assets. It's the borrowed money you use to start a business or buy an income-generating property. It's the debt that keeps giving. On the other hand, Bad Debt is the debt you accumulate to fund liabilities. It's the credit card bill from that shopping spree or the loan for the car that depreciates the moment you drive it off the lot.

Simply put, Good Debt contributes, and Bad Debt devours. It's like the difference between planting a money tree that keeps on giving versus digging a money pit that just keeps taking. That's it, right there, in its bare-bones essence. So next time you're eyeing that debt, ask yourself: is this going to be a flourishing tree or a bottomless pit?

The Power of Good Debt

In essence, good debt is a tool for wealth creation. It's taking on debt with a calculated plan of using it as a stepping-stone to generate wealth. Think about it as borrowing to invest rather than to spend.

Good debt is essentially any debt you take on to acquire assets - those things that put money into your pocket. In the grand scheme of things, good debt is all about leveraging borrowed money to create a better financial future. It's a debt that works for you, not against you. It's strategic, it's calculated, and most importantly, it's purposeful. However, remember this golden rule: good debt turns bad if you can't manage it well. Always make sure you have a solid plan for repayment and don't bite off more than you can chew.

So, let's get real with some examples.

Investment Property Mortgages

While a mortgage on your primary residence is not a form of good debt (we'll get to this in a bit), a mortgage on an investment property can be. If you're buying a property to rent out, the rental income can cover the mortgage payments, maintenance and management and potentially bring in extra profit. Over time, the property may also appreciate in value, further increasing your wealth. Now, when it comes to mortgages, they're a great tool if used correctly. They allow you to leverage other people's money to create wealth. But you've got to use them wisely.

So, you want to buy an investment property? Good. But don't just get a mortgage and buy any property. You've got to make sure that property is going to cash flow. You've got to crunch the numbers and do your homework. Can the rent you charge cover your mortgage payments, your property management, your insurance, and your maintenance, and still leave you with a profit every month? If the answer is no, then that's not the right property.

Remember this: cash flow is what matters. A property that doesn't cash flow is not an investment, it's a liability. So don't fall in love with a property, fall in love with the deal.

There are even ways to start with no money or with none of your own money. I can't even begin to list all the books you can find out there about the matter. If that's something you would like to try I recommend "Multiple Streams of Property Income" by Rob More and "No Money Down Property Investing" by Kevin McDonnell. They are both tremendous books with plenty of detailed information from people who actually practice what they preach.

So, when it comes to mortgages, don't be afraid of debt. Debt is just a tool. If you're using it to buy assets that generate income, that's good debt. Also, never put all your eggs in one basket. Diversify. Buy multiple properties. Create multiple streams of income. That's how you build wealth.

So get out there, find the deals, get the right mortgage, and start building your real estate empire. The goal isn't to just become rich. The goal is to create wealth that outlives you, wealth that can be passed down to your kids and their kids. That's the real power of real estate investing.

Business Loans

So, business loans are generally good. They can be your golden ticket, but you've got to play your cards right. Think of it like this: you're not just borrowing money, you're strategically leveraging it. You're using someone else's money to make more of your own. That's the beauty of it when you use it right.

But here's the deal: you can't just dive in without a plan. You've got to know your game. You need to figure out how you'll use this loan to ramp up income and what your repayment strategy will be. How does this loan fit into your broader business plan? These are the questions you need to answer before you even think about signing on that dotted line.

If you're in a bit of a pickle, and you're considering a loan just to keep your business above water, that's a flashing red light right there. It's a sign that something's off. If this is you, it's time to pump the brakes. Figure out why your business isn't turning a profit before you dive into more debt.

Listen, business loans are not some magic bullet that will solve all your financial headaches. They're just a tool in your entrepreneurial toolbox. They have the potential to build your business or, if used recklessly, they can tear it down. Always remember, your focus shouldn't be solely on the cash you have right now, but on your capability to generate more. Money is a means, not the end. And let's not forget; the hustle, your grit, and perseverance play a significant role in this journey.

Want a low-risk business idea? Open a doughnut shop next door to a police station.

Education Loans

First, let's get something straight. Education is critical, it's important, and it's necessary for success. But, that doesn't mean you should sink yourself into a mountain of debt to get it. In fact, one of the worst things you can do when starting off in life is strap yourself with a massive student loan.

Too many people get hung up on formal education. They think, "Oh, if I get this degree, then I'll be successful." But let me tell you something, that's a load of BS. Sure, learning is important, but the most important thing you can learn is how to think, how to adapt and how to overcome.

Now, I'm not saying you should drop out of school, okay? If you're in school, stay there. Learn. Absorb everything you can. But always remember this: a degree doesn't guarantee you anything. It's just a piece of paper. What's going to make you successful is your ability to outwork everyone else, to never quit, and to keep pushing until you get what you want.

You see, the real world, the business world, doesn't care about your degree. It cares about what you can do, and the value you can bring. So focus on increasing your value, not your debt.

Ok, if you want to become an airline pilot or a surgeon, and you've done the math and know that the return on that investment is worth it, then by all means, go the conventional way. Take a student loan, and go to university as this is the only way you'll achieve that goal. I don't think you'll get the job just by saying "I'm self-driven, highly motivated, and I read 582 books on the topic".

So, invest in yourself, in your skills, in your knowledge. But don't just rely on textbooks and lectures. Go out into the real world. Make connections. Network. Learn from experience. That's the kind of education that's going to set you apart.

And keep one thing in mind; good debt can turn bad real quick if you're not careful. It all comes back to financial responsibility, to having a plan, and to being disciplined. Don't take on debt lightly. Make sure it's for something that's going to generate income and increase your value.

The Pitfall of Bad Debt

Bad debt is the kind that doesn't generate income and will likely decrease in value over time. We're talking about credit cards, car loans, or that large personal loan you took out for a holiday or some fancy gadget. This kind of debt eats into your income because it often carries high interest rates and it doesn't help you build wealth.

OK, a high-interest loan can sometimes be a form of good debt. Like, for example, a bridge loan you take to buy a property in disrepair that mortgage lenders will not lend on. Then, have a team of renovators ready to jump in, do the minimum work necessary and make it mortgageable so you can quickly cover the bridge loan at a minimal cost. Then you can let your team finish the rest of the renovation so you can rent it out and start generating income.

But maxing out your credit card to buy the latest 60" TV only because the World Cup is coming up, is not a good use of debt. And you can't even watch it properly; you'll break your neck by the end of the game following the bloody ball. Imagine watching tennis on that screen!

Now, let's talk pitfalls. The most glaring one is the financial stress. Bad debt can be like a rock tied to your foot, constantly pulling you down. It limits your financial freedom and can even influence your day-to-day decisions.

Another pitfall is the impact on your credit score. Failure to manage and pay off your bad debts can seriously damage your creditworthiness. This can affect your ability to get good debt in the future.

Then there's the opportunity cost because the money you put towards paying off bad debt, plus the interest, is money you're not investing in your future and not using to grow your wealth. How much interest have you paid on your loans and credit cards last year? How about the year before that? What could you have done with that money? Have you ever wondered? Have you even done the math?

Finally, and maybe most importantly, there's the mindset pitfall. When you're loaded with bad debt, it's easy to develop a scarcity mindset, a constant feeling of not having enough. But to be successful, you need an abundance mindset, the belief that there's plenty out there for you to earn and achieve.

Let's have a look at some of the most common forms of bad debt.

Credit Cards

Easy to get, convenient, and highly attractive, credit cards look like freedom when you first get your hands on them and more like prison when you start paying interest.

Listen, credit card debt is like a heavyweight boxer, and you're in the ring with it. It's throwing punches at you every day in the form of interest. The longer you let it hang around, the more hits you're going to take. So, you've got to fight back.

Here's the thing: the minimum payment? That's not going to cut it. That's like trying to fight off a heavyweight with a feather. You've got to come at it with everything you've got. You need to pay more than the minimum payment, a lot more, whenever you can.

Think about it, any money you're not putting towards your credit card debt is money that's working for the credit card company, not for you. It's money that's earning them interest, not you. So, you've got to make your money work for you, not for them.

Now, if you're in a hole with credit card debt, the first thing is to stop digging. Stop adding to the debt. Cut up your cards, and start living within your means. Next, start throwing every extra penny you have at that debt. Work extra hours, sell stuff you don't need, do whatever it takes.

And here's the key: while you're fighting off this debt, you've got to educate yourself about money, like you're doing now with this book. You've got to learn how to manage your finances, how to budget, how to save, how to invest. Because once you've beaten this debt, you don't want to get back in the ring with it again.

The goal is not just to get out of debt. The goal is to build wealth. So fight off that credit card and then start using your money to make more money. That's how you win the money game.

Home Mortgages

This might sting a little, but your home mortgage is bad debt. Now, I know this goes against conventional wisdom but bear with me.

Sure, your home provides a roof over your head, but so does a rented home, and unless you're running a rental business with your pets, it's not contributing to your income. In fact, every month, you're shelling out for your mortgage, maintenance, taxes, and insurance.

Banks love to call your home an asset. But let's clear up this misunderstanding. If your house is costing you money each month rather than bringing in income, it's a liability, not an asset. And as harsh as it may sound, your home is indeed an asset for the bank, not for you. Every mortgage payment you make is money in their pocket, not yours.

And if you think a home mortgage means you own your home, try missing a few mortgage payments. You'll quickly realize who truly holds the ownership. If the bank can take it away, it's not entirely yours.

So, what's the solution here? Should you give up on homeownership entirely? No, that's not what I'm saying. But while you're trying to get out of debt or to create wealth you should invest in assets that help you achieve your goals, not liabilities that slow you down. You can own as many as you want once you're out of debt and you can truly afford it. Owning a home can be a valuable part of your financial strategy, but not when you're just getting off the ground.

Consider other ways to invest your money. Real estate is a great tool, but I'm talking about income-producing properties. That could be multi-unit residential properties, commercial properties, or even single-family homes that you rent out. Also, consider other forms of investment, like starting a business or investing in stocks and bonds. Diversification is key.

Car Loans

And now, let's talk about the elephant in the room, or more appropriately, the 2-tonne chunk of metal in the driveway. A car loan is the poster child for bad debt.

Picture this: You buy a brand-new car for 40k, right? You finance it because if you can drop 40k in cash on a brand-new car, you're probably not reading this book. At the time of writing the interest rates for car finance are between 8% and 12% if you have a good credit history. So if we use 10% for our example, that finance adds about 37% to the total cost over five years. Then, the moment you drive it off the lot, your shiny new toy drops about 30% in value. So you end up paying 55k for a car that's worth 28k the second you leave the dealership. Not exactly a smart investment, right?

How about flipping the pancake now? What if you bought two cars instead of one? Both used, both 2-3 years old and of course on finance. You rent one out to someone who does Uber or other forms of TAXI service and the rent pays the finance for both cars leaving you with a car for free. Who would want to rent a car from you when they could get one on finance themselves? Someone who doesn't have a good enough credit score to qualify for a car loan.

Now, what would you rather have, a brand spanking new car for 50k or a 2-year-old one for free? And if your answer is not the latter then you can close this book and fill out the application form for personal bankruptcy, because that is where you are going.

Store Cards and Catalogue Credit

These might seem like a sweet deal, easy to get, easy to use, but believe me, they're a debt trap in disguise. They lure you in with the enticing promise of "Buy now, pay later", but let's be real, it often translates to "Enjoy now, weep later".

Let me break it down for you. When you buy something on credit, you're not just delaying payment, you're often committing to high interest rates and fees. And if you can't make the payments? Late fees. Missed payment fees. Your debt can spiral out of control before you even realize what's happening.

Now, about those "interest-free" deals. They sound great, right? But there's no such thing as free money. If you read the fine print, you'll often find that these deals are only interest-free for a limited time. Miss the deadline to pay off the balance, and suddenly you're hit with all the accrued interest. And trust me that can pack a punch.

Remember this: credit is not an extension of your income. It's not extra money; it's borrowed money. And borrowed money always has a cost.

So, the next time you're tempted by a store card or catalogue credit, ask yourself: Do I really need this? Can I truly afford it? Am I prepared to pay the cost of borrowing this money?

The path to financial freedom isn't paved with easy credit and debt. It's built on sound financial decisions, disciplined spending, and action. Don't let the allure of instant gratification trap you in a cycle of debt. Be smart, be proactive, and take control of your finances.

Summary and Key Takeaways

As we wrap up this chapter, let's take a moment to reflect on the journey we've taken together. We've delved into the world of debt, stripped away the complexities, and laid bare the fundamental truths. We've discovered that not all debt is created equal and that understanding the difference between good and bad debt is crucial to your financial success.

We've learned that good debt, when used wisely, can be a powerful tool for wealth creation. It's the kind of debt that puts money in your pocket, whether it's a business loan used to expand your operations, a mortgage on an investment property, or an education loan that enhances your skills and increases your earning potential. But even good debt can turn sour if not managed properly. It's essential to have a solid plan for repayment and to never bite off more than you can chew.

On the flip side, we've also learned about the pitfalls of bad debt. This is the kind of debt that drains your resources and impedes your journey towards financial freedom. It's the credit card bills, the car loans, the store cards, and the personal loans for unnecessary luxuries. These debts offer no return on investment and can quickly spiral out of control if not kept in check.

The key takeaway from this chapter is that debt, like any tool, is only as good or bad as the person wielding it. It's not inherently evil or beneficial. It's a means to an end, and it's up to you to decide whether that end is financial freedom or financial ruin.

Every financial decision you make is a step towards or away from your goal of financial freedom. When you choose to take on debt, ask yourself: Is this good debt or bad debt? Is it going to generate income, or is it going to keep me shackled to monthly payments with no return?

As we move forward, remember the lessons learned in this chapter. Use debt wisely. Invest in assets, not liabilities. Make your money work for you, not against you. And above all, maintain a winner's mindset. Financial freedom is not just about having money; it's about having control over your money. It's about making informed decisions, taking calculated risks, and reaping the rewards of your hard work and smart choices.

So, as you close this chapter and prepare to embark on the next phase of your financial journey, remember this: Debt is a tool, and you are the craftsman. Use it wisely, and you can construct a future of wealth, prosperity, and financial freedom. Use it recklessly, and you risk building a future of financial instability and stress. The choice is yours. Choose wisely, and the path to financial freedom is yours to walk.

Chapter 4

Credit Scores

These three-digit numbers might seem mysterious, but they're an important part of your financial health. Your credit score is a reflection of you in the financial world. It's your reputation, your trustworthiness, your ticket to financial freedom or a life of struggle. Understanding your credit score is key to navigating the financial landscape.

Now, you might be thinking, "But I pay my bills on time, isn't that enough?" Well, I hate to break it to you, but it's not. It's a start, sure, but there's a whole lot more to it than that. Your credit score is calculated based on a bunch of factors, including how much debt you have, how long you've had credit, and even how many times you've applied for new credit.

Even if you're doing everything right, one small slip-up can send your score plummeting. Late payment? Your score takes a hit. High balances on your credit cards? Your score takes a hit.

Applied for a new credit card or loan? You guessed it, your score takes a hit.

But this isn't a doom and gloom story. It's a wake-up call. It's a call to action and a chance for you to take control of your financial future. In this chapter, we're going to break down the ins and outs of credit scores. We're going to demystify the process, cut through the jargon, and give you the tools you need to boost your score and unlock financial opportunities for you.

What is a Credit Score?

So, what exactly is a credit score? Let's break it down. A credit score, in its simplest form, is a numerical representation of your creditworthiness. Think of it as a financial report card or a scorecard that captures your past behaviour with credit. It's a tool that lenders use to gauge the risk they take when they lend you money.

In the UK, credit scores range from 0 to 999. These scores are then categorised into five bands: very poor, poor, fair, good, and excellent. Each band represents a level of trust that lenders are likely to have in your ability to repay borrowed money. The higher your score, the more creditworthy you appear to potential lenders.

Across the pond in the US, credit scores operate on a slightly different scale, ranging from 300 to 850. Similar to the UK, these scores are divided into categories, ranging from bad to excellent.

But a credit score is more than just a number. It's a snapshot of your financial discipline, a reflection of your credit history. It takes into account several factors from your financial past: your payment history, the amount of debt you have, the length of your credit history, the types of credit you've used, and how often you've applied for new credit.

In essence, your credit score is a financial fingerprint, unique to you. It tells a story about your relationship with money, about how you've managed debt, and how you've met your financial obligations. It's a crucial part of your financial identity, one that can open doors to new opportunities or close them, depending on how well you've managed your credit.

How Credit Scores Are Calculated

Credit scores are calculated based on several factors. These include your payment history (do you pay your bills on time?), credit utilisation (how much of your available credit are you using?), length of credit history (how long have you been borrowing?), the types of credit you use (loans, credit cards, mortgages, etc.), and recent applications for credit. Each of these factors is weighted differently, contributing to your overall score.

Let's break down these factors:

Payment History:

This is the big one, the main player when it comes to your credit score. It's a whopping 35% of your total score, so it's a big deal. Basically, it's like your financial report card, showing if you've been good about paying your bills on time.

Every time you pay a bill, it's like getting a gold star. But if you're late, or worse, you default on a loan or declare bankruptcy, it's like a big, red F on your report card. And trust me, those red Fs can really drag your score down.

Late payments are bad news because they show you're not great at juggling your debts. Defaults are even worse, they're like saying, "I give up, I can't pay this." And bankruptcies, well, they're the nuclear option. They can blow your credit score to smithereens.

So, think of your payment history as your financial life story. It's not just about what you're doing right now, but how you've handled your money over time. Keeping it clean is super important if you want a good credit score. After all, it's the first thing lenders check out when deciding if they should lend you money and at what rate.

Credit Utilisation:

This one's a bit like how much of your credit card limit you're using. It's the ratio of what you owe to your total credit limit, and it's a biggie, making up about 30% of your score.

Think of it like this: if your credit limit is a pizza, your credit utilisation is how many slices you've eaten. If you've eaten most of the pizza (high credit utilisation), it doesn't look so good. It's like you're really hungry for credit, and that can make lenders nervous. But if you've only had a couple of slices (low credit utilisation), it looks like you're in control and not relying too much on credit.

So, lower credit utilisation is better for your score. It's like showing you can have a whole pizza in front of you, but you're not going to eat it all in one go. As a general rule, try to keep your credit utilisation below 30%. That's like having a 10-slice pizza and only eating 3 slices. It shows you're not maxing out your credit, and that's a good look to lenders.

Length of Credit History:

This is a pretty significant chunk of your credit score, making up around 15% of the total. It's not just about how long you've had credit, but it's a bit more nuanced than that. It considers the age of your oldest credit account, the age of your newest credit account, and the average age of all your accounts. This average gives a more balanced view of your overall credit history.

Why do lenders care about all this? Well, a longer credit history gives them a better picture of your financial behaviour. It's like a track record of how you've managed your money over time. If you've been consistent and responsible, it shows lenders that you're less of a risk. They like to see that you've got some experience under your belt when it comes to handling credit. It's like a financial resume of sorts, and the longer it is, the more confident they feel about lending to you.

Credit Mix:

So, this is all about the different kinds of credit you've got under your belt. It's like a financial buffet - credit cards, student loans, car loans, mortgages, you name it. This whole mix makes up about 10% of your credit score, so it's not something to ignore.

Now, you might be thinking, why does it matter if I have different types of credit? Well, having a diverse credit mix is actually a good thing for your score. It's like showing off your financial flexibility. If you've got a credit card, a car loan, and a mortgage, and you're managing all of them well, it sends a positive signal to lenders.

It's like saying, 'Hey, I can juggle different types of credit and not drop the ball.' This gives lenders confidence that you can handle various types of debt. It's not just about having credit, but showing that you can manage different kinds of credit responsibly. So, while it's not the biggest piece of the credit score pie, it's still a slice worth paying attention to.

New Credit:

Alright, so this one's all about how many new accounts you've been opening and how many hard inquiries you've got on your record. Hard inquiries are basically when a lender takes a peek at your credit because you've applied for some new credit. This could be a new credit card, a car loan, a mortgage, or anything else that involves borrowing money. This whole new credit business accounts for about 10% of your credit score.

Now, you might be thinking, 'So what if I open a bunch of new accounts?' Well, here's the thing: opening a lot of new accounts in a short time can actually ding your score. It's kind of like going on a credit spree, and it can make you look risky to lenders.

Think about it this way: If you're suddenly applying for a lot of credit, lenders might think you're in a financial bind or planning to go on a spending spree. It's like seeing someone at a buffet piling their plate high with food - it makes you wonder if they're really going to eat all that, or if they're just biting off more than they can chew.

So, while it's not a huge part of your score, it's still important. It's all about showing lenders that you're not just grabbing at any credit you can get, but that you're managing your credit responsibly.

But credit score is not static. It's a dynamic number that can change as new information is added to your credit report. So, every financial decision you make, from paying your bills on time to opening a new credit card, can impact your score.

Understanding how your credit score is calculated gives you the power to influence it. By focusing on the factors you can control, like making timely payments and keeping your credit utilisation low, you can work towards building a strong credit score. It's like knowing the rules of a game. Once you know how to play, you can start making strategic moves to win.

How to Access Your Credit Score

Knowing your credit score is an essential part of managing your financial health, just like knowing your weight is part of managing your physical health.

In the UK, you can access your credit score for free through several services. These include Experian, Equifax, and TransUnion, which are the three main credit reference agencies in the country. Each of these agencies may have a slightly different score for you, as they use different scoring models and may have different information about your credit history.

In the US, you're entitled to one free report from each of the three major credit bureaus (Experian, Equifax, and

TransUnion) per year, thanks to the Fair Credit Reporting Act. This means you can check your credit score for free three times a year. You can request these reports through AnnualCreditReport.com, the only official site explicitly directed by Federal law to provide them.

There are also various online services that provide free credit scores. These include platforms like Credit Karma, Credit Sesame, and others. These services often provide additional features, such as credit monitoring and personalized tips to improve your credit score.

Remember, checking your own credit score is considered a soft inquiry and doesn't impact your score. This is different from a hard inquiry, which occurs when a lender checks your credit when you apply for credit and can slightly lower your score.

Accessing your credit score isn't a one-time thing. It's a good idea to check your score regularly to keep track of your financial health. Regular checks can help you catch any sudden changes in your score, which could indicate errors in your credit report or potential fraud.

However, while knowing your credit score is important, it's also crucial to remember that it's just one aspect of your financial health. A high credit score doesn't necessarily mean you're in good financial shape, and a low score doesn't mean you're in bad shape. It's just one tool of many that can help you understand and manage your finances.

How to Improve Your Credit Score

Now that we've covered what a credit score is, how it's calculated, and how to access it, let's take all that theory and put it into practice.

Improving your credit score is not a sprint; it's a marathon. It's not about quick fixes or overnight transformations; it's about consistent, responsible financial behaviour over time. But with patience, discipline, and the right strategies, you can work towards a better credit score. Here's how:

Pay Your Bills on Time: This is the most important factor in your credit score. Make sure you're paying all your bills on time, every time. This isn't just about credit card bills or loan payments; it also includes your utility bills, rent, and even mobile phone contract. Consider setting up direct debits to ensure you never miss a payment.

Keep Your Credit Utilisation Low: Try to use no more than 30% of your available credit. So, if you have a credit limit of £3,000, try not to carry a balance of more than £1,000. This shows lenders that you can manage your credit responsibly and aren't reliant on borrowing.

Don't Apply for Credit Too Often: Every time you apply for credit, it results in a hard inquiry on your credit report, which can lower your score. Try to only apply for new credit when you really need it.

Maintain a Healthy Credit Mix: Having a mix of different types of credit, like a credit card, a car loan, and a mortgage, can be beneficial for your credit score. However, this doesn't mean you should take on debt you don't need; it's more about showing that you can manage different types of credit responsibly.

Check Your Credit Report Regularly: Regularly check your credit report for any errors or fraudulent activity. If you spot anything that doesn't look right, report it to the credit reference agency immediately. They have a duty to investigate and correct any errors.

Register on the Electoral Roll: In the UK, being registered on the electoral roll provides proof of address and can boost your credit score. If you're not a UK citizen, you can add a note to your credit report to confirm your residential status and show stability.

Build Your Credit History: If you're new to credit or have a thin credit file, consider taking out a credit builder credit card. These cards have low limits and high-interest rates, but if you use them responsibly and pay off your balance in full each month, they can help you build up a credit history.

Remember, improving your credit score is a journey, not a destination. You'll have to build and maintain good financial habits over the long term. It might take time to see significant improvements, but every step you take towards better financial behaviour is a step in the right direction.

So, don't be discouraged if your score doesn't skyrocket overnight. Keep making those on-time payments, keep your credit utilisation low, and keep checking your credit report. Over time, these positive habits will pay off, and you'll see your credit score start to climb. And with a higher credit score, you'll have access to better financial opportunities and more financial freedom.

Seven Myths About Credit Scores

In the world of credit scores, myths and misconceptions abound. These can lead to unnecessary stress and misguided financial decisions. So, let's set the record straight and debunk some of these common misconceptions.

Myth 1: Checking Your Credit Score Lowers It.

This is one of the most persistent myths about credit scores and it likely arises from the fact that there are two types of credit inquiries: soft and hard inquiries.

Soft Inquiries are checks that you or others make that do not affect your credit score. When you check your own credit score or report, it's considered a soft inquiry. Soft inquiries also occur when a company checks your credit for promotional purposes, like pre-approved credit card offers. Even potential employers might do a soft inquiry as part of a background check. These types of inquiries are not considered by credit scoring models and therefore do not affect your credit score.

Hard Inquiries are the inquiries that can potentially lower your credit score. Hard inquiries occur when a lender or credit card issuer checks your credit when you apply for a loan or credit card. These inquiries are recorded on your credit report and can slightly lower your credit score for a short period of time. This is because potential lenders view numerous hard inquiries within a short time frame as a sign of financial distress, indicating that you may be a higher credit risk.

It's important to note that not all hard inquiries will significantly impact your credit score. If you're shopping for a specific type of loan (like a mortgage or auto loan) and you do your rate shopping within a short period of time (typically 14 to 45 days, depending on the scoring model), credit scoring models will typically count all those inquiries as a single inquiry. This is to encourage consumers to shop around for the best rates without being penalized.

In conclusion, checking your own credit score is a soft inquiry and does not impact your credit score. It's a good practice to regularly monitor your credit report and score to understand your credit health, spot any errors, and track your progress if you're working to improve your score. It's a crucial part of financial literacy and can help you maintain good credit health.

Myth 2: You Only Have One Credit Score.

The belief that each individual only has one credit score is a common misconception. In reality, each person has multiple credit scores, and these scores can vary based on several factors.

Different Credit Reference Agencies: In the UK, there are three main Credit Reference Agencies (CRAs) - Experian, Equifax, and TransUnion. Each of these agencies collects information about your credit history and generates a credit report. While they all collect similar types of information (like your payment history, the amount of debt you have, and the length of your credit history), the information they collect might not be exactly the same. For example, a certain lender might report to Experian and TransUnion, but not Equifax. This can result in slightly different credit reports and, therefore, different credit scores.

Different Scoring Models: Each of the CRAs uses its own model to calculate your credit score, and these models can produce different results. For example, Experian scores range from 0-999, Equifax from 0-700, and TransUnion (formerly Callcredit) from 0-710. These scores are categorised into bands (e.g., 'poor', 'fair', 'good', 'excellent') which can also differ between agencies.

Time of Inquiry: Your credit score can also change over time, even from day to day. This is because the information in your credit report changes as new information is added or old information is removed. For example, if you pay off a credit card or loan, that will be reflected in your credit report and could cause your score to change.

In the United States, the situation is similar but with some differences. You also have three main CRAs - Experian, Equifax, and TransUnion. However, the scoring models used are primarily FICO and VantageScore, both of which range from 300-850. Just like in the UK, the scores can vary based on the information each CRA has and the scoring model used.

Myth 3: You Need to Carry a Credit Card Balance to Build Credit.

This is a dangerous myth that can lead to unnecessary interest charges. Here's a more detailed explanation:

Credit Utilisation and Payment History: Two of the most important factors in your credit score are your credit utilisation and your payment history. Credit utilisation is the percentage of your available credit that you're using. A lower credit utilisation rate is generally better for your credit score. Payment history refers to whether you pay your bills on time. Late or missed payments can have a negative impact on your credit score.

Paying Off the Balance: Contrary to the myth, you do not need to carry a balance on your credit card to build credit. In fact, consistently paying off your balance in full each month is a good way to demonstrate responsible credit use. It shows lenders that you can manage your credit well and can lead to improvements in your credit score over time.

Interest Charges: Carrying a balance on your credit card from month to month won't boost your credit score, but it will lead to interest charges. Credit card interest rates are typically quite high, so carrying a balance can quickly lead to significant interest charges. These charges can add up over time, making it more difficult to pay off your balance and potentially leading to more serious credit problems.

Building Credit: The best way to build credit is to use your credit card regularly for purchases you can afford, and then pay off the balance in full each month. This shows that you're using credit responsibly, which can help improve your credit score. It's also a good idea to keep your credit utilisation low, as high utilisation can be a red flag to lenders.

In conclusion, the idea that carrying a balance on your credit card is necessary or beneficial for your credit score is a myth. In reality, the best way to build credit is to use your credit responsibly, keep your credit utilisation low, and pay your balance in full each month. This approach will help you avoid unnecessary interest charges and build a strong credit history.

Myth 4: Closing Old Credit Cards Will Improve Your Score.

Closing old or unused credit cards can actually hurt your score by reducing your available credit and increasing your credit utilisation ratio. Let me explain:

Credit Utilisation Ratio: One of the key factors that influence your credit score is your credit utilisation ratio, which is the percentage of your available credit that you're using. Closing an old or unused credit card reduces your available credit, which can increase your credit utilisation ratio if you have balances on other cards. A higher credit utilisation ratio can negatively impact your credit score.

Length of Credit History: Another important factor in your credit score is the length of your credit history. Lenders like to see a long history of responsible credit use. In this context, older credit accounts are beneficial because they extend your credit history. Closing these accounts can shorten your credit history, which can potentially lower your credit score.

Account Mix: Having a mix of different types of credit (like credit cards, car loans, and mortgages) can also positively impact your credit score. Closing a credit card account could reduce this mix, which might have a negative effect on your score.

Annual Fees: While it's usually better to keep old accounts open, there can be exceptions. If an old credit card has high annual fees and you're not using the card, it might make financial sense to close the account. However, you should consider the potential impact on your credit score before making this decision.

So, closing old or unused credit cards can potentially harm your credit score. It's usually better to keep old accounts open, especially if they have a long history or a high credit limit, and they're not costing you money in annual fees.

Myth 5: Your Salary Affects Your Credit Score.

I heard this a number of times and it makes me cringe every time I hear it. Your income has no direct impact on your credit score. It's all about how you manage your money, not how much you make. However, lenders may consider your income when deciding whether to approve you for credit. Let me break it down for you:

Income and Credit Score: In both the UK and the US, your income does not directly affect your credit score. Credit scores are calculated based on the information in your credit report, which includes your payment history, the amount of debt you have, the length of your credit history, the mix of credit types you have, and your recent applications for credit. Your income is not part of this information.

Money Management: What does impact your credit score is how you manage your money. Paying your bills on time, keeping your credit utilisation low, having a long history of credit use, maintaining a mix of different types of credit, and not applying for new credit frequently are all behaviours that can help improve your credit score.

Income and Lending Decisions: While your income doesn't affect your credit score, it can affect your ability to get credit. Lenders often consider your income when deciding whether to approve you for credit. They do this to assess your ability to repay the money you borrow. A higher income might make it more likely that you'll be approved for credit, but it won't affect your credit score.

Debt-to-Income Ratio: In addition to your credit score, lenders may also look at your debt-to-income ratio, which is the percentage of your income that goes towards paying your debts each month. A lower debt-to-income ratio indicates that you have a good balance between your income and debt, which can make you more attractive to lenders.

So, although lenders may consider your income when deciding whether to approve you for credit, that is more to ensure you have the means to repay the borrowed amount and it has nothing to do with your credit score.

Myth 6: Credit Scores Take Years to Change.

The belief that credit scores take years to change is a common misconception. In reality, your credit score is a dynamic number that can change as new information is added to your credit report. Here's a more detailed explanation:

Dynamic Nature of Credit Scores: Credit scores are not static; they are dynamic and can change over time. They are calculated based on the information in your credit report, which is continually updated as new data is reported by your creditors. This means your credit score can change as often as the information in your credit report changes.

Significant Improvements: While it's true that making significant improvements to your credit score can take time, this is usually in the context of recovering from major negative events like bankruptcy or foreclosure. These events can significantly lower your credit score, and it can take several years for your score to recover.

Small Changes: On the other hand, small changes can happen relatively quickly. For example, if you pay down a high credit card balance, this will reduce your credit utilisation ratio, which is a key factor in your credit score. This can lead to an improvement in your credit score within a month or two. Similarly, if you correct an error on your credit report, this can also lead to a quick improvement in your score.

Regular Monitoring: Regularly monitoring your credit report and score can help you understand how your financial behaviour affects your score and can help you make decisions that will improve your credit health over time.

In conclusion, credit scores can change relatively quickly based on the information in your credit report. While significant improvements may take time, small positive changes in your financial behaviour can lead to improvements in your credit score in a short period of time. It's all about understanding the factors that influence your credit score and managing your credit responsibly.

Myth 7: A Bad Credit Score Will Haunt You Forever.

Everyone makes financial mistakes, but a low credit score isn't a life sentence.

Duration of Negative Information: In the UK, most negative information will fall off your credit report after six years. This includes late payments, defaults, and even more serious events like bankruptcy. In the US, most negative information stays on your credit report for seven years, although some bankruptcies can remain for up to ten years.

Diminishing Impact: The impact of negative information on your credit score diminishes over time. This means that a late payment from five years ago will have less impact on your score than a late payment from last month. So even if you've made mistakes in the past, they won't affect your credit score forever.

Rebuilding Credit Score: It's entirely possible to rebuild your credit score by adopting good financial habits. This includes paying all your bills on time, keeping your credit utilisation low, maintaining a mix of different types of credit, and applying for new credit sparingly. Over time, these positive behaviours can help to improve your credit score, even if you've had problems in the past.

So, contrary to the myth, a bad credit score will not haunt you forever. Negative information will eventually fall off your credit report, and you can rebuild your credit score by adopting good financial habits. It's all about understanding the factors that influence your credit score and managing your credit responsibly.

Understanding the truth about credit scores can empower you to make smarter financial decisions. So, don't let these myths hold you back. Your credit score is in your hands, and with the right knowledge and actions, you can influence it for the better. Remember, a credit score is just a snapshot of your financial health at a specific point in time. It's not a judgment of your worth or a prediction of your future. It's just a tool, and like any tool, it's most effective when you know how to use it.

Summary and Takeaways

As we wrap up this chapter, let's take a moment to reflect on what we've learned. We've demystified the concept of credit scores, delved into their calculation, and explored how to access and improve them. We've also debunked some common myths that often cloud our understanding of credit scores.

Understanding your credit score is like having a roadmap to your financial health. It shows you where you stand today and points you in the direction you need to go to reach your financial goals. It's a powerful tool in your financial toolkit, one that can open doors to new opportunities and help you build a solid financial foundation.

But remember, while your credit score is important, it's not the be-all and end-all of your financial health. It's just one piece of the puzzle. Your financial health is also about having a budget and sticking to it, saving for the future, and making informed financial decisions. It's about understanding the difference between wants and needs and making choices that align with your financial goals.

Improving your credit score isn't an overnight process. It requires patience, discipline, and consistent effort. But every step you take towards improving your credit score is a step towards greater financial freedom. It's a journey, and like any journey, there will be ups and downs, twists and turns. But with the knowledge you've gained in this chapter, you're well-equipped to navigate this journey.

So, as we close this chapter, I encourage you to take what you've learned and put it into action. Check your credit score, understand what's impacting it, and take steps to improve it. Remember, your credit score is not set in stone. It's a living, breathing thing that changes over time. And with the right actions, you can shape it, mould it, and improve it.

Chapter 5

The Battle Plan

Alright, we're about to dive into the heart of this book. This chapter is your battle plan, your roadmap to financial freedom. It's the blueprint you need before you start building your debt-free future.

Why do you need a battle plan? Because jumping headfirst into the battlefield without a clear strategy is a recipe for disaster. It's like trying to navigate through a dense forest without a compass. You'll end up lost, confused, and overwhelmed.

But with a clear plan, you'll have a sense of direction. You'll know exactly what steps you need to take and in what order. You'll have a clear vision of your destination, and you'll know exactly how to get there.

This battle plan will also provide clarity in moments of confusion. When you're feeling overwhelmed by your debt, when you're not sure what to do next, you can always come back to this chapter. It will serve as your guiding light, leading you out of the darkness and towards financial freedom.

The plan consists of 5 major points all of which will be explained in much greater detail in the following seven chapters. What I'm trying to do in this chapter is to provide you with a clear and solid scaffolding for all the information in the following seven chapters. This will avoid confusion and overwhelm, and you will know exactly where in your battle plan each chapter fits.

So let's roll up our sleeves and get to work.

Step 1: Assess Your Situation

Before you can start tackling your debt, you need to know what you're up against. That's why the first step in your battle plan is to assess your financial situation. This is about getting a clear, honest picture of where you stand right now. It's about facing the reality of your debt, no matter how scary it might be.

First, take a look at your income. How much money are you bringing in each month? This includes your salary from your job, any income from side hustles or part-time work, social support, and any other sources of income you might have. Be sure to include regular income, not just one-off payments.

Then, consider your monthly expenses. How much are you spending on housing, food, transportation, utilities, entertainment, and other expenses? And don't forget to include your debt payments in your expenses.

Now, list all your debts, including credit cards, student loans, car loans, mortgages, and any other debts you might have. Write down the total amount you owe, the interest rate, and the minimum monthly payment for each debt.

And finally, move on to your assets. This includes money in your bank accounts, investments, real estate, and other valuable items you own. Knowing your assets is important because it gives you a sense of your overall financial health and can help you decide on the best strategy for paying off your debt.

Once you've gathered all this information, take a moment to reflect on it. What does it tell you about your financial situation? Are you living within your means, or are you spending more than you earn? How much of your income is going towards debt payments? Are there any changes you need to make to get your finances back on track?

This step is not about judging yourself or feeling bad about your situation. It's about understanding where you are so you can figure out how to get where you want to go. So be honest with yourself, but also be kind to yourself (yes I know; I can't believe I just said that either). You're taking the first step towards financial freedom, and that's something to be proud of.

Step 2: Create a Budget

Alright, so now that you've got a clear picture of where you're at financially, it's time to get down to business and create a budget. Think of this as your financial game plan. It's going to be your roadmap to keeping track of what's coming in and what's going out, and most importantly, it's going to be your strategy for tackling your debt.

First things first, you're going to want to list out all your monthly expenses. I'm talking everything - your rent or mortgage, utilities, groceries, transportation, and even your Netflix subscription. And let's not forget those nights out or your morning coffee runs. Basically, if you're spending money on it, it goes on the list. And don't forget to include your minimum debt payments. I'm not talking about how much you usually pay, just the bare minimum you're required to pay.

Once you've got all that down, it's time to do some math. Subtract your expenses from your income. This will give you an idea of how much dough you've got left over each month that you can put towards your debt, on top of those minimum payments.

Now, if you're looking at that number and it's not as much as you'd like, or worse, it's in the red, don't freak out. Remember, this is just the first step. We're going to figure out how to work with what you've got and make it better in the next steps. So, take a deep breath, and let's get ready to tackle this together.

Step 3: Increase Your Income

Now, this is where things get exciting. This is where you start to take control and push the boundaries of what's possible.

Increasing your income is one of the most effective ways to pay off your debt faster. It's simple math. The more money you have coming in, the more money you can put towards your debt. But how do you go about increasing your income?

First, look at your current job. Are there opportunities for a raise or promotion? If you've been at your job for a while and have been performing well, it might be time to have a conversation with your boss. Don't be afraid to advocate for yourself. Show them the value you bring to the company and make your case.

Then see if you may have an opportunity to earn extra income at work providing a service to the people you come in contact through you current job. See, it's not all about quitting your job and jumping head first in uncharted waters. Try to increase the efficiency of the time you already allocate to work.

Next, consider starting a side hustle. This could be anything from freelance work to starting your own online business. The possibilities are endless. The key is to find something you enjoy and are good at. That way, it won't feel like work, and you'll be more likely to stick with it.

You could also consider investing as a way to increase your income. This could be investing in the stock market, real estate, or even starting your own business. But remember, investing involves risk, so it's important to do your research and consider seeking advice from a financial advisor.

Finally, don't forget about passive income. This is income that you earn without having to actively work for it. This could be from renting a room in your house, dividends from investments, or royalties from a book or invention.

Remember, there's no limit to your income potential. It's all about how much value you can provide. So get creative, think outside the box, and start increasing your income today!

Step 4: Reduce Expenses

Alright, now that we've talked about boosting your income, let's flip the coin and talk about reducing your expenses. This is the other side of the equation, and it's almost as important.

Reducing your expenses means more of your income can go towards paying off your debt. It's about making your money work harder for you. But here's the key: it's not about depriving yourself or living in misery. It's about making smart choices and getting the most value out of your money.

Start by taking a good, hard look at your budget. Where is your money going? Are there areas where you're spending more than you need to? Maybe you're eating out too often, or you're paying for subscriptions you don't use. These are the low-hanging fruits, the easy cuts you can make without drastically changing your lifestyle.

Next, look at your bigger expenses. Can you find a cheaper place to live? Can you negotiate lower rates on your insurance or internet bill? Can you refinance your mortgage or car loan to get a lower interest rate? These changes require more effort, but they can also have a big impact on your budget.

Now, here's the caution: don't cut your expenses to the point where it becomes counterproductive. You don't want to be living in a constant state of deprivation, because that's not sustainable. You'll end up miserable, and you're more likely to give up on your debt repayment plan.

For example, don't cut your grocery budget so much that you end up eating unhealthy food, because that could lead to higher medical bills or time off sick down the road. Don't cancel your gym membership if working out is your main form of stress relief. And don't skimp on maintenance for your car or home, because that could lead to more expensive repairs in the future.

The goal, here, is to reduce expenses, not to eliminate all joy from your life. You need to find a balance between living a life you enjoy and reaching your financial goals. So make smart cuts, but also make sure you're taking care of yourself and investing in your future.

Step 5: Decide on Your Approach

So you've assessed your situation, created a budget, worked on increasing your income, and reduced your expenses. Now, it's time to decide on your approach to tackling your debt. This is a crucial step because the strategy you choose can significantly impact how quickly you can become debt-free.

There are several strategies you can choose from, and the best one for you depends on your personal circumstances and preferences.

Debt Snowball Method:

This method involves paying off your debts from smallest to largest, regardless of the interest rate. The idea is that by paying off smaller debts first, you'll gain momentum and motivation to tackle the larger ones. This method can be very effective if you're motivated by quick wins.

Debt Avalanche Method:

This method involves paying off your debts from highest interest rate to lowest, regardless of the balance. The idea is that by paying off high-interest debts first, you'll save money in the long run. This method can be very effective if you're motivated by saving money.

Now, what if neither of these methods seems suitable for your situation? That's where debt consolidation and refinancing options come into play.

Debt Consolidation:

This involves taking out a new loan to pay off all your existing debts. You then make one monthly payment towards this new loan. The benefit of this approach is that it simplifies your payments and can potentially lower your interest rate. However, it's important to note that you're not actually reducing your debt, just restructuring it. You'll still need to make regular payments and be disciplined about not accumulating more debt. The good part is that the new loan may be taken on a longer term and although you may pay more interest overall, servicing the loan may require smaller payments. This can be a good option if you're in a tight spot. Better still, if most of your debt is in credit cards with high interest rates, a consolidation loan will most likely come with a lower rate and you win both ways.

Refinancing:

This involves replacing your existing loan with a new one that has more favourable terms, such as a lower interest rate. This can be a good option if your credit score has improved since you took out your original loan, or if interest rates have dropped. However, refinancing often involves fees, so you'll need to make sure the savings outweigh the costs.

The best approach is the one that you can stick to. It's not about which method is theoretically the best, but which one works best for you. So consider your options, decide on your approach, and then commit to it.

Summary and Takeaways

So there you have it; your five step battle plan. Everything you do with your finances has to agree with and fit somewhere in this plan. If it doesn't then it is probably not worth doing.

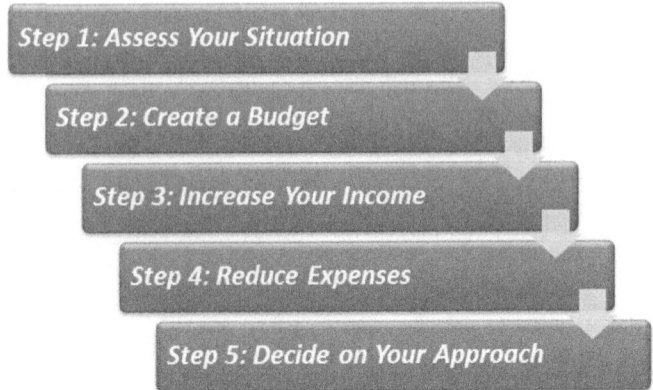

Remember, this battle plan is not set in stone. It's a living, breathing document that should evolve as your financial situation changes. So don't be afraid to come back to this chapter and make adjustments as needed.

And most importantly, remember to take action. A plan is only as good as the action that follows it. So get out there and start conquering your debt! You've got this!

Chapter 6

Assess Your Financial Situation

Now it's time to take a good, hard look at your financial situation. This isn't the time for sugar-coating or denial. It's the time for honesty and action. This is the first step in your battle plan, and it's crucial to get a clear picture of where you stand right now. Assessing your financial situation is about more than just knowing how much money you have in the bank. It's about understanding your overall financial health, including your income, expenses, debts, and assets. You need to know where your money is coming from, where it's going, and how it's being used.

Why is this important? Because understanding your financial situation is the first step towards taking control of your finances. It's the foundation upon which you can build a plan to pay off your debt, save for the future, and achieve financial freedom.

Without a clear understanding of your financial situation, it's like trying to navigate a maze in the dark. You need it so you can make informed decisions, set realistic goals, and track your progress towards achieving them.

Now, let's talk about net worth. Your net worth is a snapshot of your financial health at a specific point in time. It's calculated by subtracting your liabilities (what you owe) from your assets (what you own). If your assets are greater than your liabilities, you have a positive net worth. If your liabilities are greater than your assets, you have a negative net worth.

Understanding your net worth is important because it gives you a broader perspective of your financial situation. It's not just about how much money you have in the bank, but also about how your wealth is distributed. Do you have a lot of assets but also a lot of debt? Or do you have few assets but also little debt? Knowing your net worth can help you understand these dynamics and make smarter financial decisions.

You can't improve what you don't measure, so let's measure!

Income

Your income is the backbone of your financial health. It's the starting point for any financial plan. You need to know exactly how much money you have coming in each month. This isn't just your salary from your day job. It includes any side hustles, rental income, dividends, alimony, child support, social security benefits, and any other source of income you might have. Understanding your income is crucial because it sets the boundaries for your budget, your spending, and your ability to save and invest.

There are several different types of income you might have:

Salary: This is the money you earn from your job. It's usually paid on a regular basis, such as weekly, bi-weekly, or monthly.

Hourly Wages: If you're paid by the hour, your income can vary depending on how many hours you work each week.

Bonuses: Some jobs offer bonuses based on performance or company profits.

Freelance Income: If you do freelance work or have a side hustle, this is the money you earn from those activities.

Passive Income: This is income that you earn without having to actively work for it. It could come from investments, rental properties, royalties, benefits or other sources.

Here's a simple table you can use to list your sources of income:

Source of income	Amount per month
Salary / Hourly Wages	
Overtime	
Bonuses	
Freelance Income	
Passive Income	
Other	
Total	

Table 1

It's also important to understand the stability of your income. Is it fixed, meaning it's the same amount every month? Or is it variable, meaning it can change from month to month? Knowing this can help you plan your budget and manage your money more effectively.

Now, you need to understand the difference between gross income and after-tax income. Your gross income is the total amount of money you earn before taxes and other deductions. Your after-tax income, also known as your net income or take-home pay, is the amount you have left after taxes and other deductions are taken out. It's your after-tax income that you'll use to pay your expenses and save for the future, so that's the one you should use in all calculations.

Understanding your income is the first step towards taking control of your finances. It's the foundation upon which you can build a plan to pay off your debt, save for the future, and achieve financial freedom. So take the time to really understand your income and what it means for your financial situation.

Expenses

Expenses are the other side of the financial equation. They're the money that you spend on everything from housing and food to entertainment and debt payments. Understanding your expenses is just as important as understanding your income because it shows you where your money is going.

There are several different types of expenses you might have:

Fixed Expenses: These are expenses that stay the same from month to month. They include things like rent or mortgage payments, car payments, insurance premiums, and any subscriptions or memberships you might have.

Variable Expenses: These are expenses that can change from month to month. They include things like utilities, groceries, dining out, entertainment, and personal care items.

Periodic Expenses: These are expenses that don't occur every month, but that you need to plan for. They include things like annual memberships, vehicle maintenance, medical expenses, and holiday gifts.

Here's a simple table you can use to list your expenses:

Expense Category	Amount per Month
Housing	
Groceries	
Transportation	
Utilities	
Entertainment	
Insurance	
Other	
Total	

Table 2

When listing your expenses, it's important to be thorough and honest. Don't forget to include small expenses or expenses that don't occur every month. These can add up and have a big impact on your budget.

Now, I know you can't predict medical expenses or a temporary illness that may leave you unable to work and earn for a number of days, especially if you're self-employed. What you can do in this case is to estimate based on the average of your last three or four years.

Once you've listed all your expenses, add them up to find your total monthly expenses. Then, compare this to your total monthly income. Are you spending more than you earn? If so, you'll need to find ways to cut back on your expenses or increase your income.

Understanding your expenses is a crucial part of assessing your financial situation. It can help you identify areas where you can save money, prioritize your spending, and make a plan to pay off your debt and achieve your financial goals. So take the time to really understand your expenses and what they mean for your financial situation.

Debts

The word alone can make us cringe. But it's time to face them head-on. It's crucial to have a clear understanding of how much debt you have, what kind of debt it is, and what it's costing you. This includes credit card debt, student loans, car loans, personal loans, payday loans, and any other type of debt you might have.

For each debt, you should know the total amount you owe, the interest rate, the minimum monthly payment, and the repayment term. This will help you prioritize your debts and develop a repayment strategy, which we'll discuss in later chapters.

Remember, debts are not just numbers. They're chains holding you back from your financial freedom. It's time to break free. Every payment is a step towards your freedom.

Here's a simple table you can use to list your debts:

Type of Debt	Total Amount Owed	Interest Rate	Minimum Monthly Payment
Credit Card			
Student Loan			
Mortgage			
Car Loan			
Personal Loan			
Other			
Total			

Table 3

When listing your debts, be sure to include all relevant information. The total amount owed is how much you currently owe. The interest rate is the percentage of the loan amount that you're charged each year. The minimum monthly payment is the smallest amount you can pay each month without being considered delinquent.

Understanding your debts is the first step towards paying them off. Once you know how much you owe, who you owe it to, and what terms you agreed to, you can create a plan to pay off your debt and achieve financial freedom. So take the time to really understand your debts and what they mean for your financial situation.

Assets

Assets are the things you own that have value. They can be a source of income, a store of wealth, or both. Understanding your assets is an important part of assessing your financial situation because it gives you a fuller picture of your financial health.

Here are some common types of assets you might have:

Cash: This includes the money in your current and savings accounts, as well as any physical cash you have.

Investments: This includes stocks, bonds, mutual funds, and other investment accounts.

Retirement Accounts: This includes state pension and workplace pension in the UK or 401(k)s and IRAs in the US, and other retirement savings accounts.

Real Estate: This includes your primary residence (confusion to be cleared), as well as any rental properties or vacation homes you own.

Vehicles: This includes cars, trucks, motorcycles, boats, and other vehicles.

Personal Property: This includes furniture, electronics, jewellery, and other valuable items.

Here's a simple table you can use to list your assets:

Type of Asset	Value
Current (Checking) Account	
Savings account	
Investments	
Real Estate	
Vehicles	
Personal Property	
Other	
Total	

Table 4

When listing your assets, be sure to consider their current market value, not just what you paid for them. The market value is the amount you could reasonably expect to sell the asset for today.

Understanding your assets is a crucial part of assessing your financial situation. It can help you identify resources you can use to pay off debt, save for the future, or invest in new opportunities. So take the time to really understand your assets and what they mean for your financial situation.

Calculating Your Net Worth

Your net worth is a snapshot of your financial health. It's the difference between what you own (your assets) and what you owe (your liabilities). Calculating your net worth can give you a clear picture of your overall financial situation and help you track your progress towards your financial goals.

Here's the basic formula for calculating your net worth:

Net Worth = Total Assets - Total Liabilities

To calculate your net worth, you'll need to add up all your assets and all your liabilities. Then, subtract your total liabilities from your total assets. I trust you don't need another table for that.

Your net worth can be positive or negative. If it's positive, it means you own more than you owe. If it's negative, it means you owe more than you own.

It's important to note that your net worth is not a measure of your value as a person. It's simply a tool to help you understand your financial situation.

Calculating your net worth on a regular basis can help you track your progress over time. You can see how your net worth changes as you pay off debt, save and invest money, or acquire new assets.

Understanding your net worth is a crucial part of assessing your financial situation. It can help you make informed decisions about how to manage your money, set financial goals, and measure your progress towards those goals. So take the time to calculate your net worth and understand what it means for your financial situation.

Creating Your Cash Flow Statement

Your cash flow statement is a document that shows how money moves in and out of your personal economy over a certain period of time. It's a crucial tool for understanding your financial health and planning for the future.

Creating a cash flow statement involves tracking your income and expenses over a certain period of time, usually a month. You'll list all your sources of income and all your expenses, then subtract your total expenses from your total income to find your net cash flow.

Here's the basic formula for calculating your cash flow:

Net Cash Flow = Total Income - Total Expenses

Your net cash flow can be positive or negative. If it's positive, it means you're bringing in more money than you're spending. If it's negative, it means you're spending more money than you're bringing in.

Understanding your cash flow is crucial for managing your finances. It can help you identify areas where you can cut back on spending, opportunities to save more money, and strategies for paying off debt faster.

Creating a cash flow statement can also help you plan for the future. By understanding how money flows in and out of your personal economy, you can make informed decisions about things like investing, buying a home, starting a business, or retiring.

So take the time to create a cash flow statement and understand what it means for your financial situation. It's a powerful tool that can help you take control of your finances and achieve your financial goals.

Looking to the Future

Looking to the future is a crucial part of assessing your financial situation. It involves considering upcoming life changes, planning for future expenses, and setting financial goals.

Are you planning to get married, have children, change careers, or retire in the near future? These life changes can have a big impact on your financial situation, so it's important to plan for them.

Are you planning to buy a home, pay for college tuition, travel, or cover healthcare costs in the future? These expenses can be significant, so it's important to start saving for them now.

What are your financial goals? Do you want to pay off debt, save for retirement, build an emergency fund, or achieve financial independence? Setting clear, specific financial goals can help you stay motivated and make progress towards your financial dreams.

I know you don't want to see another table, but I think this one might be very useful:

Future Plan or Goal	Estimated Cost	Target Date

Table 5

When you're looking to the future, it's important to be realistic but also to dream big. Don't limit yourself to what you think is possible based on your current situation. Instead, envision the life you want to live and the financial situation you want to have, then make a plan to achieve it. That's why I said this table is very important; it makes you think big and it pushes you to seek alternative income streams.

Looking to the future is a crucial part of assessing your financial situation. It can help you make informed decisions, set financial goals, and plan for the life you want to live. So take the time to envision your future and what it means for your financial situation.

Utilizing Financial Tools

In today's digital age, there are countless financial tools and resources available that can make managing your finances easier and more efficient. These tools can automate calculations, track your spending, and provide visualizations of your financial data, making it easier to understand and manage.

Here are some types of financial tools you might consider using:

Budgeting Apps:

These applications are designed to help you manage your money more effectively. They allow you to create a personalized budget, track your income and expenses, and provide insights into your spending habits.

- ***Mint:*** Mint is a free app that brings together all your financial accounts, bills, and more. It allows you to see where you're spending, where you can save money, and where you can budget better. It also offers free credit score checks and reminders for upcoming bills.

- ***YNAB (You Need A Budget):*** YNAB is a budgeting app that follows a zero-based budgeting principle, meaning every penny has a job. It helps you plan for every expense and offers real-time access to data, which can be shared with a partner. There is a cost associated with this app after the initial free trial.

- ***PocketGuard:*** PocketGuard is an app that focuses on showing you how much disposable income you have at any given time, helping you to avoid overspending. It categorizes and organizes your expenses, monthly bills and subscriptions into clear, beautiful pie charts.

Investment Platforms:

These platforms provide a space for you to invest your money in various assets, track your investment performance, and manage your portfolio.

- ***Robinhood:*** Robinhood is a commission-free investing platform. It allows you to invest in stocks, ETFs, options, and cryptocurrencies all in one place. It also offers a premium paid account with additional features.

- ***Vanguard:*** Vanguard is an investment platform known for its low-cost mutual funds and ETFs. It offers a wide range of investment options, including retirement accounts and education savings accounts.

- ***Fidelity:*** Fidelity is a comprehensive and responsive platform that allows you to invest in a wide range of options including stocks, bonds, mutual funds, and retirement accounts. It also offers extensive research tools and resources.

Debt Repayment Tools:

These tools help you create a plan to pay off your debts, taking into account factors like interest rates and repayment periods.

- ***Unbury.me:*** Unbury.me is a free tool that allows you to list out your debts, and then uses either the 'snowball' (smallest balances first) or 'avalanche' (highest interest rates first) method to show you how to pay them off.

- ***Debt Snowball Calculator:*** This tool, often found on various financial advice websites, helps you to implement the debt snowball method, where you pay off your smallest debts first to create momentum as you knock out larger debts.

Retirement Planning Tools:

These tools help you plan for your retirement by calculating how much you need to save and offering strategies to meet your retirement goals.

- ***Personal Capital's Retirement Planner:*** This tool allows you to build, manage, and forecast your retirement in one place. It takes into account your income, spending, and savings to provide a comprehensive retirement plan.

- ***Vanguard's Retirement Nest Egg Calculator:*** This tool helps you determine the likelihood of your savings lasting through your retirement. It uses Monte

Carlo simulation to show possible outcomes in your portfolio.

Net Worth Trackers:

These tools help you calculate your net worth (the difference between your assets and liabilities) and track it over time.

- ***Personal Capital:*** In addition to its retirement planning tool, Personal Capital offers a comprehensive net worth tracker. It allows you to link all your financial accounts to get a complete picture of your net worth.

- ***Mint:*** Along with its budgeting features, Mint also provides a net worth tracking feature. It automatically updates and displays your net worth as you pay down debt and your investments grow.

This is by no means an extensive list. There are plenty more apps out there for you to try and use. Some tools are free, while others require a subscription. Some are simple and easy to use, while others offer more advanced features. Choose the tools that best fit your needs and will help you achieve your financial goals.

Utilizing financial tools can make managing your finances easier and more efficient. They can provide valuable insights, automate tedious tasks, and help you stay organized. So take the time to explore the financial tools available and find the ones that work best for you.

Summary and Key Takeaways

In this chapter, we've embarked on a comprehensive journey to assess your financial situation. We've delved into the importance of understanding your income, expenses, debts, and assets. We've also discussed the significance of calculating your net worth and creating a cash flow statement. Looking to the future, we've considered upcoming life changes, planned for future expenses, and set financial goals. Lastly, we've explored various financial tools that can assist you in managing your finances more effectively.

Assessing your financial situation is not a one-time task, but a continuous process. It's about maintaining an ongoing awareness of your financial health and making informed decisions based on that awareness. It's about taking control of your finances, setting realistic goals, and tracking your progress towards achieving them.

The purpose of this assessment is not to judge or criticize, but to enlighten and empower. It's about shedding light on your financial reality, no matter how daunting it may seem. It's about taking that first crucial step towards financial freedom.

As we conclude this chapter, I encourage you to reflect on what you've learned and apply it to your own financial situation. Use the tables and tools provided to get a clear picture of where you stand financially. Be honest with yourself, be thorough, and don't shy away from the hard truths.

Remember, knowledge is power. The more you understand about your financial situation, the better equipped you'll be to take control of it. So, take this knowledge and use it as a stepping stone towards financial freedom. The journey may be challenging, but the destination is worth it.

Chapter 7

Create a budget

Alright, it's time to roll up your sleeves and get down to business. We're going to talk about creating a budget. Now, before you roll your eyes and start thinking about how boring and restrictive budgets are, let me stop you right there. A budget is not a financial straitjacket that's going to suck the joy out of your life. It's a tool, a roadmap that's going to guide you to your financial goals. It's about making sure your hard-earned money is going where it needs to go and not just disappearing down a black hole of impulse buys and unnecessary expenses.

Let's get one thing straight: A budget is not about deprivation. It's not about telling you that you can't have the things you want. It's about helping you prioritize your spending so that you can have the things that are most important to you. It's about making conscious decisions with your money, instead of wondering where it all went at the end of the month.

Think of your budget as a spending plan. It helps you take control of your money, instead of letting your money control you. It's a way for you to say, "This is my money, and this is how I choose to use it."

Creating a budget can feel overwhelming, especially if you've never done it before. But don't worry; I'm going to walk you through it step by step. And don't expect your first budget to be perfect, it won't be. It's going to take some tweaking and adjusting to find a budget that works for you. The important thing is to just get started.

To help you visualize the process, I'll be including graphs and tables throughout this chapter. For example, I'll provide a pie chart to show you how to allocate your income to different categories. This will give you a starting point for creating your own budget.

I'll also provide a budget template that you can use to track your income and expenses. This template will be a simple spreadsheet where you can input your numbers and see how they add up.

In essence, a budget is a tool to serve you. It should reflect your values, your goals, and your lifestyle. It's not about cutting out all the fun in your life; it's about making sure you have the money for the fun things while also taking care of your responsibilities and working towards your financial goals.

So, are you ready to take control of your money and start budgeting? Let's do this!

Types of Budgets

Let's dive into the different types of budgets. There's no one-size-fits-all when it comes to budgeting. What works for your best friend or your neighbour might not work for you. The key is to find a budgeting method that fits your income, expenses, and financial goals. Let's take a look at some of the most popular budgeting methods out there.

Zero-Based Budget

Zero-based budgeting (ZBB) is a method of budgeting where every penny of income is assigned to a specific expense category, so the total income minus total expenses equals zero. This doesn't mean you spend all your money, but rather that you're giving each dollar a specific job, whether that's for living expenses, savings, or investments.

The zero-based budget is excellent for those who need a detailed plan for their money. It's a proactive approach that requires you to plan your spending in advance, rather than reacting to expenses as they come up. This can help you avoid impulse purchases and stay on track with your financial goals.

One of the main benefits of ZBB is that it can help you identify areas where you're overspending. By allocating a specific amount to each category, you can easily see where your money is going and where you might need to cut back. This can be especially helpful for discretionary spending categories, like dining out or entertainment, which can often be the source of overspending.

Another advantage of ZBB is the ability to make adjustments as needed. If you find that you're consistently overspending in one category and underspending in another, you can reallocate funds accordingly. This flexibility allows you to adapt your budget to your changing needs and priorities.

However, it's important to note that ZBB does require a significant amount of time and effort to maintain. You need to track every penny you spend and regularly review and adjust your budget. This can be time-consuming, but many people find it worthwhile for the control it gives them over their finances.

ZBB can also be a powerful tool for saving money and paying off debt. By assigning a job to every penny, you ensure that you're regularly contributing to your savings goals and making progress on your debt repayment. This can help you build a strong financial foundation and work towards financial independence.

Lastly, ZBB promotes financial discipline. It encourages you to live within your means and make conscious decisions about your spending. This can lead to healthier financial habits and a more sustainable lifestyle.

In conclusion, zero-based budgeting is a comprehensive and proactive approach to managing your finances. It can provide a clear picture of your spending habits, help you identify areas for improvement, and allow you to adjust your budget to meet your financial goals. However, it does require a commitment of time and effort to implement and maintain.

Here's a simple template for a zero-based budget:

Category	Budget Amount	Actual Amount	Difference
Income			
Housing			
Food			
Transportation			
Savings			
Debt Repayment			
Other			
Total			

Table 6

The 50/30/20 Rule

The 50/30/20 rule is a simple and straightforward budgeting method that divides your after-tax income into three broad categories: needs, wants, and savings or debt repayment. This method is particularly useful for those who prefer a less detailed approach to budgeting compared to methods like zero-based budgeting.

Needs (50%): The largest portion of your budget goes to necessities. These are the things you can't live without and include housing (like rent or mortgage payments), food, transportation (such as car payments, gas, and public transit costs), utilities (like electricity, water, and heating), and health insurance. It's important to note that what constitutes a "need" can vary from person to person, but generally, these are the expenses that ensure your health and safety.

Wants (30%): This category includes non-essential expenses that enhance your lifestyle. These might include dining out, entertainment, shopping, hobbies, personal care, vacations, and other discretionary expenses. The key, with this category, is understanding that these are items or services you could live without if necessary. They're not your bare-bones expenses, but they're the things that make life more enjoyable and provide a sense of reward.

Savings and Debt Repayment (20%): The final portion of your income should be allocated towards savings and debt repayment. This includes contributions to your emergency fund, retirement savings like a 401(k) or IRA, and paying down debt. This category is crucial for your financial health and future. By consistently allocating money to this category, you're investing in your future financial stability and independence.

The 50/30/20 rule is a great starting point for people new to budgeting or those who prefer a less detailed approach. It provides a simple framework that can help you make sure you're not overspending in any one area. However, it's also flexible enough to be adjusted based on your personal circumstances.

For example, if you live in a high-cost-of-living area, you might need to allocate more than 50% of your income to needs. Or, if you have high levels of debt, you might choose to put more than 20% towards savings and debt repayment.

So the 50/30/20 rule is a straightforward and effective budgeting method that can help you manage your money in a balanced way. It ensures that you're meeting your basic needs, enjoying your life, and investing in your future, all at the same time.

Here's a pie chart to visualize the 50/30/20 rule:

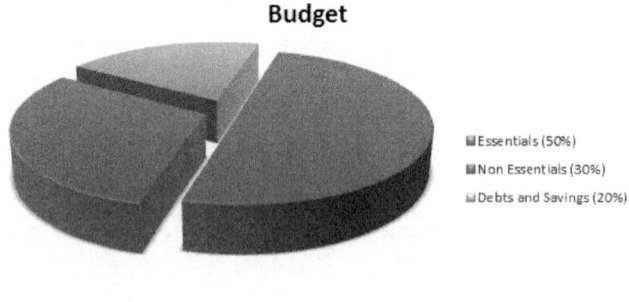

Fig. 1

The Envelope System

The envelope system is a budgeting method that involves dividing your cash into different envelopes for each spending category. This method is particularly beneficial for those who struggle with overspending, as it provides a tangible, visual way to control spending.

One of the main advantages of the envelope system is its tangibility. Physically allocating cash to different envelopes can make the concept of budgeting more concrete. When you can see and touch the money you have for each category, it can make your budget feel more real and easier to stick to.

The categories you choose for your envelopes can be as broad or as specific as you like. Common categories might include housing, food, transportation, and entertainment, but you can also include categories for things like clothing, personal care, or hobbies. The key is to make sure you're covering all your regular expenses.

Here's how you might set up an envelope system:

- Housing envelope (£1,000): This envelope would cover your rent or mortgage payment, as well as any other housing-related costs like homeowners or renters insurance.

- Food envelope (£300): This envelope would cover all your food expenses for the month, including groceries, dining out, and any other food-related costs.

- Transport envelope (£200): This envelope would cover your transport costs, such as fuel for your car, public transit fares, or maintenance and insurance costs.

- Entertainment envelope (£100): This envelope would cover any entertainment expenses, like going to the movies, concerts, or other events.

Once the money in an envelope is gone, you can't spend any more in that category until the next month. This can help curb impulse spending and encourage you to think more carefully about your purchases.

The envelope system is flexible and can be adjusted to fit your personal circumstances and financial goals. If you find that you're consistently running out of money in one envelope but have a surplus in another, you can reallocate funds as needed.

The best budgeting method for you depends on your personal circumstances and financial goals. The envelope system is just one method, and it may not be the best fit for everyone. It's important to spend some time researching different methods and choose the one that fits your lifestyle and goals the best.

In conclusion, the envelope system is a simple and tangible budgeting method that can help you control your spending and stay within your budget. It's a great option for those who prefer a hands-on approach to budgeting and need a visual reminder of their spending limits.

Setting Financial Goals

Setting financial goals is a crucial part of budgeting. It's like setting a destination before you start a journey. Without a clear destination, you're just wandering aimlessly. But with a clear goal in mind, you have a direction to move towards. You know where you're going and you can plan the best route to get there.

Financial goals can be short-term, medium-term, or long-term. Short-term goals are things you want to achieve in the next year or so, like saving for a vacation or paying off a credit card. Medium-term goals might be things you want to achieve in the next 5 years, like saving for a down payment on a house. Long-term goals are things you want to achieve in 10 years or more, like saving for retirement or paying off your mortgage.

Here are some steps to help you set effective financial goals:

- **Be Specific:** Your goals should be clear and specific. Instead of saying "I want to save money," say "I want to save £5,000 for a pilot training course to get your Private Pilot Licence." This gives you a clear target to aim for and it may provide some good extra income to help pay your debt sooner.

- **Make it Measurable:** Your goals should be measurable so that you can track your progress. If your goal is to save £5,000 for the course, you can measure your progress by how much you've saved each month.

- **Ensure it's Achievable:** Your goals should be achievable. It's good to aim high, but make sure your goals are realistic and within your reach. If there's always too much month left at the end of your money, it might not be achievable to save £5,000 in a year. But saving £1,000 might be doable with some changes.

- **Keep it Relevant:** Your goals should be relevant to your life and your values. If you don't care about flying, saving for a pilot training course might not be a relevant goal for you. But saving for a down payment on a house or for your child's education might be.

- **Set a Time-bound Target:** Your goals should be time-bound. This means setting a deadline for when you want to achieve your goal. If you want to save £5,000 for the course, when do you want to have this money saved by? In a year? In two years? Set yourself a deadline because that sense of urgency will spark your creativity to do more in less time.

Your financial goals are personal to you. They should reflect what you want to achieve in your life, not what someone else thinks you should achieve. And don't be afraid to adjust your goals as your circumstances change. The most important thing is that your goals inspire you to take action and make progress towards financial freedom.

Creating Your Budget

You're now going to create your budget. This is your financial blueprint, your roadmap to financial freedom. It's going to guide your spending and saving decisions, and it's going to help you stay on track to reach your financial goals.

Start by gathering all your financial information. This includes your income, fixed costs, variable expenses, and any other financial obligations. You've already done some of this work in the previous chapter, so you're already ahead of the game.

Now add up all your sources of income. This includes your salary, any side hustles, rental income, dividends, etc. Make sure to use your net income (after taxes and deductions). This is the money you actually have to work with each month.

Next, list out all your fixed costs. These are expenses that don't change from month to month. This includes things like rent or mortgage, car payments, insurance premiums, and any other recurring bills.

Now, list out your variable expenses. These are costs that can change from month to month. This includes things like groceries, fuel, entertainment, and personal care items.

Remember to allocate money for debt repayment and savings. This is a crucial part of your budget. It's how you're going to get out of debt and build financial security.

Now that you've listed out all your income and expenses, it's time to do some math. Subtract your total expenses from your total income. If you end up with a positive number, great! That's money you can put towards your financial goals. If you end up with a negative number, don't panic. This just means you need to make some adjustments. Look for areas where you can cut back or ways you can increase your income.

Don't forget that a budget is not set in stone. It's a living document that should evolve with your needs and circumstances. Review it regularly and make adjustments as needed. The goal is to create a budget that works for you and helps you reach your financial goals.

Creating a budget might seem like a lot of work, but it's worth it. It gives you control over your money and puts you in the driver's seat. So take the time to create a budget and commit to sticking to it. Your future self will thank you.

Implementing Your Budget

Alright, you've got your budget. You've done the hard work of crunching the numbers and setting your financial goals. Now comes the fun part: implementing your budget. This is where the rubber meets the road, where your plans become actions.

The first step in implementing your budget is to start tracking your spending. This is crucial because it gives you a clear picture of where your money is going. You can do this manually by keeping receipts and logging your expenses in a notebook or spreadsheet. Or, you can use a budgeting app or software that automatically tracks your spending for you.

Make a habit of checking in with your budget regularly. This could be weekly, bi-weekly, or monthly, depending on what works best for you. Regular check-ins allow you to see how you're doing and make adjustments as needed. Are you overspending in one category? Are you on track to meet your financial goals? Regular check-ins keep you accountable and help you stay on track.

Setbacks are another thing you will have to prepare for, as they are a normal part of life. Maybe your car breaks down and you have an unexpected repair bill. Or maybe you lose your job and your income drops. When setbacks happen, don't panic. Take a deep breath, assess the situation, and adjust your budget as needed. The goal of your budget is to help you navigate through financial challenges, not to add to your stress.

And don't forget to celebrate. Implementing a budget can be tough, especially in the beginning. That's why it's important to celebrate small wins along the way. Did you stick to your grocery budget this month? Celebrate! Did you pay off a credit card? Celebrate! Celebrating small wins keeps you motivated and makes the budgeting process more enjoyable.

Implementing your budget is a crucial step in your financial journey. It's where your plans become actions. It might be challenging at times, but remember, you're doing this for a reason. You're doing this to achieve financial freedom. So stick with it, stay focused, and don't forget to celebrate your progress along the way.

Reviewing and Adjusting Your Budget

So you've done the hard work of creating your budget and implementing it. But guess what? Your job isn't over yet. A budget isn't a set-it-and-forget-it kind of thing. It's a living, breathing document that needs to be reviewed and adjusted regularly. Let's talk about how to do that.

First things first, you need to be reviewing your budget regularly. This could be weekly, bi-weekly, or monthly, depending on what works best for you. The point is to stay on top of your spending and make sure you're sticking to your budget.

During your budget review, you should be looking at:

- How much you've spent in each category

- Whether you've gone over or under budget in any categories

- Any unexpected expenses that came up

- How much you've been able to save or put towards debt

After reviewing your budget, the next step is to make adjustments as needed. This could mean increasing or decreasing the budgeted amount for certain categories, adding new categories, or removing categories that are no longer relevant.

The goal of your budget is to help you reach your financial goals. If your budget isn't working for you, don't be afraid to make changes. Your budget should be flexible and adaptable to your changing needs and circumstances.

As you're reviewing and adjusting your budget, always keep your financial goals in mind. Your budget is a tool to help you reach these goals. If your current budget isn't helping you progress towards your goals, it might be time for a bigger adjustment.

Finally, don't be too hard on yourself if your budget isn't perfect. Budgeting is a skill that takes time to master. There will be months where you overspend and months where you underspend. The important thing is that you're making an effort to manage your money better. Keep learning, keep adjusting, and keep moving forward.

Reviewing and adjusting your budget is a crucial part of successful budgeting. By staying on top of your spending, making adjustments as needed, and keeping your financial goals in mind, you can create a budget that truly works for you.

Summary and Key Takeaways

Alright, let's wrap this up. We've covered a lot of ground in this chapter, so let's take a moment to summarize the key points and takeaways.

Budgeting is a crucial tool for managing your money effectively. It helps you understand where your money is going, make informed financial decisions, and work towards your financial goals. If you're serious about getting out of debt and achieving financial freedom, you need to be serious about budgeting.

There are several different types of budgets you can use, including the Zero-Based Budget, 50/30/20 Rule, and Envelope System. The best budgeting method for you depends on your personal circumstances and financial goals.

Setting clear, specific financial goals is a key part of successful budgeting. Your goals give you something to work towards and help guide your budgeting decisions. Remember to make your goals SMART - Specific, Measurable, Achievable, Relevant, and Time-bound.

Your budget should account for all your income and expenses. This includes your fixed costs (like rent and utilities), variable expenses (like groceries and transportation), and discretionary spending (like dining out and entertainment).

Your budget should also include allocations for debt repayment and savings. How much you allocate to each will depend on your financial goals and current situation.

Creating your budget is just the first step. You also need to implement your budget and stick to it. This might involve tracking your spending, using budgeting tools or apps, and regularly checking in on your budget.

Don't forget to budget for irregular or unexpected expenses. This can help you avoid going into debt when these expenses come up.

Finally, remember to regularly review and adjust your budget. Your budget should be flexible and adaptable to your changing needs and circumstances.

Budgeting is a skill that takes time to master, and it's okay if your budget isn't perfect right away. The important thing is that you're making an effort to manage your money better. Keep learning, keep adjusting, and keep moving forward. You've got this!

Chapter 8

Increase Your Income

If you're serious about getting out of debt and achieving financial freedom, you've got to understand one thing: You can't just sit around, cut coupons, and hope that your debt will magically disappear. It won't. You can't shrink your way to greatness. It's like trying to lose weight by thinking about dieting with a full English breakfast on your plate. It's not going to work.

Personally, I believe this step to be more important than all the other steps put together. Think about it; if you were able to increase your income five times, you wouldn't need to cut expenses, you wouldn't need to budget, and you wouldn't even need to assess your financial situation. You would just have five times more money coming in and you'd be done with your debts and financial worries in no time at all.

So you've got to increase your income. That's right; you need more cash flowing into your bank account. It's simple math.

The more you earn, the more you can throw at your debt, and the faster you'll be sipping cocktails on a beach somewhere without a financial worry in the world.

Now, I know what you're thinking. "I'm stuck in a job that I hate and I don't know how to increase my income." Well, that's why you're reading this book, isn't it? In this chapter, you're going to be served a buffet of ways to boost your earnings. We'll talk about everything from climbing the corporate ladder (or jumping off it entirely) to starting a side hustle, to making money while you sleep with passive income.

So buckle up, because you're in for a rocket ride. And remember, I'm not here to cuddle you. This is going to require effort, creativity, and a willingness to step outside your comfort zone. But trust me; the view is much better from up here; so let's get started.

Career Advancement

Alright, let's talk about your job. Yes, that thing you drag yourself to every day. It's currently your main source of income, and it's pretty important in this whole "getting out of debt and achieving financial freedom" game.

Now, you might be comfortable in your current role. You know the ropes, you get along with your co-workers, and the coffee in the break room isn't half bad. But let me ask you this:

When was the last time you got a raise? If you have to think about it, it's been too long.

Here's the deal. If you've been in your role for a while and you're doing a good job, you should be earning more. It's time to put on your big kid pants and ask for a raise. Do your research, know your worth, and present your case. Show your boss how you've added value to the company. And keep in mind that the worst they can say is no.

Then see if you may have an opportunity to earn extra income at work by providing a service to the people you come in contact with through your current job. If you work in a sweets shop, for example; could you design and sell colouring books or story books for kids? See, you don't necessarily have to quit your job and jump head-first into uncharted waters. Try to increase the efficiency of the time you already allocate to work.

But what if there's no room for growth in your current job? Well, then it might be time to jump ship. Look for opportunities in other companies or even other industries. Changing jobs is one of the fastest ways to increase your income. It might be scary, but so is being stuck in debt forever.

And let's not forget about upskilling. In today's fast-paced world, learning never stops. Whether it's taking an online course, getting a certification, or going back to school, improving your skills can make you more valuable in the job market. Think of it as an investment in yourself. After all, you're the most important asset you have.

So, stop settling for your current income level. It's time to step up, take charge, and get paid what you're worth. Your debt-free future depends on it.

Side Hustles

Now let's move on to one of my favourite topics: side hustles. I know what you're thinking. "I'm already working 40 hours a week, and now you want me to take on more work?" Well, yes. That's exactly what I'm saying.

Look, I get it. After a long day at work, all you want to do is kick back, watch some TV, and forget about the world. But you're not here to do what's easy. You're here to do what's necessary. And sometimes, what's necessary is hustling a little harder.

Firstly, you need to understand that a side hustle is not just about the money. It's about personal growth, learning new skills, and exploring your passions. It's about taking control of your financial future and creating opportunities for yourself.

For instance, if you're a talented writer, you could start a blog or offer freelance writing services. You could write about anything you're passionate about, from travel to technology, fashion to food. This not only allows you to earn some extra cash but also helps you improve your writing skills, build a portfolio, and establish a presence in the industry.

If you're into photography, you could start selling your photos online on platforms like Shutterstock or Adobe Stock. You could also offer your services for events or portrait photography. This side hustle can help you improve your photography skills, build a portfolio, and establish a network of clients.

For those who are tech-savvy, you could offer your services as a freelance web developer or start creating and selling your own software or apps. This way you'll keep on top of the latest technology trends, improve your coding skills and increase your income at the same time.

If you love teaching, you could start tutoring in your free time. This could be anything from academic subjects to music lessons, and language classes to yoga instruction. You could offer these services in person or online earning some extra cash and also improving your teaching skills.

For those who are crafty, you could start selling handmade products online on platforms like Etsy. This could be anything from jewellery to home decor, clothing to artwork. This side hustle not only provides a source of income but also allows you to express your creativity and establish a brand.

The key to a successful side hustle is passion. If you love what you do, it won't feel like work. It will be something you look forward to, something that brings you joy and fulfilment. And who knows? It might just turn into a full-time gig.

So, stop scrolling through social media in your free time and start hustling. Your wallet will thank you. And who knows? You might just find your true calling along the way.

Passive Income

Alright, let's talk about the dream: making money while you sleep. Sounds too good to be true, right? Well, buckle up!

Passive income is indeed a dream for many, but it's important to remember that it doesn't come without effort. It requires an initial investment of time, money, or both. However, once the groundwork is laid, the income can continue to flow with minimal effort on your part.

One of the most popular examples of passive income is investing in the stock market. This could be through dividend-paying stocks, where you receive a portion of the company's earnings at regular intervals. Or, it could be through growth stocks, where you buy stocks at a low price and sell them at a higher price.

Another example is real estate investment. This could be through rental properties, where you earn income from rent paid by tenants. Or, it could be through real estate investment trusts (REITs), where you invest in a portfolio of properties and earn income from the profits.

If you have a knack for creating digital content, you could create an online course or an eBook on a topic you're knowledgeable about. Once the course or eBook is created and published, you can earn income every time someone purchases it.

Affiliate marketing is another great source of passive income. This involves promoting other people's products or services and earning a commission every time someone makes a purchase through your referral link.

If you're a software developer, you could create an app or a software program. Once the app or program is developed and launched, you can earn income every time someone downloads it or purchases a license.

Creating a blog or a YouTube channel is another way to generate passive income. Once you have a substantial amount of content and a steady stream of traffic, you can earn income through advertising revenue, sponsored posts, or product partnerships.

Investing in peer-to-peer lending platforms is another way to generate passive income. These platforms allow you to lend money to individuals or small businesses in return for interest payments.

The key to successful passive income is diversification. Don't put all your eggs in one basket. Instead, create multiple streams of passive income. This not only increases your earning potential but also reduces the risk.

And if you don't know how to do any of the above, let me remind you that you have the great library of Alexandria multiplied 1000 times at your fingertips. Everything and anything you need to know is available online and, in most cases, for free. You can find tutorials for any crazy thing that crosses your mind on YouTube. And if it seems daunting, remember that anything you haven't yet mastered seems more difficult and complicated than it actually is.

So, stop trading your time for money and start building passive income streams. It might take time and effort, but trust me, waking up to see that you've made money in your sleep? There's nothing sweeter.

Selling Unused Items

It's time for a little tough love. You see that loft full of stuff you haven't touched in years? Or that garage filled with tools you used once for a project you never finished? It's not just clutter, it's cash. That's right, your junk could be someone else's treasure.

Selling unused items is one of the easiest ways to make some quick cash. And let's face it, we all have stuff lying around that we don't use or need. That guitar you bought during your "I'm going to be a rock star" phase? Sell it. Those designer shoes you wore once and then realized they were incredibly uncomfortable? Sell them. Even broken electronics have a market. Your old broken laptop, phone, tablet or satnav will sell like hotcakes on eBay.

Ok, this may not be the key to riches, but at least it could provide the starting capital for a side hustle or seed funds to generate passive income. And thanks to the internet, selling your stuff has never been easier. Platforms like eBay, Craigslist, and Facebook Marketplace are perfect for this. You can reach thousands of potential buyers with a few clicks.

Here's the key to successful selling: good photos, competitive pricing, and honest descriptions. Take clear, well-lit photos from multiple angles. Price your items fairly by checking what similar items are selling for. And be honest about the condition of the item. If there's a scratch or a dent, mention it in the description. Your honesty will build trust with buyers.

So, take a look around your house. What items are just collecting dust? Turn them into cash and use that money to pay down your debt or invest in your future. One man's trash is another man's treasure. And right now, your treasure is buried under a pile of unused stuff. It's time to dig it out.

Renting Out Property

If you have a spare room, a second car, or even a parking spot you're not using, you could be sitting on a gold mine.

Renting out property is a fantastic way to generate extra income. It's like having a mini business that doesn't require much work once you've set it up. And the best part? There are platforms out there that make it incredibly easy.

Take Airbnb, for example. If you have a spare room or a holiday home that's often empty, you can rent it out to travellers. You set the price, the rules, and the availability. Airbnb handles the payments and provides insurance in case anything goes wrong.

Or maybe you live in a city and have a parking spot but no car. You'd be surprised how much people are willing to pay for parking. List it on a platform like JustPark and watch the bookings roll in.

If you have a boat that's often sitting idle, you could rent it out on a platform like GetMyBoat. This allows you to earn income from your boat when you're not using it. You set the price and the availability, and GetMyBoat handles the bookings and payments.

If you have a workspace or a studio that's often unused, you could rent it out to artists, freelancers, or small businesses. Platforms like Peerspace and ThisOpenSpace make it easy to list your space and handle the bookings and payments.

Even your car can make you money. If you often leave it sitting in the driveway, consider renting it out on a platform like Turo. It's like Airbnb, but for cars.

But being a landlord, even a part-time one, comes with responsibilities. You'll need to keep your property in good shape and be responsive to your renters' needs. And don't forget to check local laws and regulations, as well as how they might impact your taxes.

So, take a look at what you've got and consider how it could be making you money. Your path to financial freedom could be closer than you think.

Investments

Alright, let's get serious for a moment. If you're not investing, you're leaving money on the table. I'm not talking about playing the lottery or betting on the horses. I'm talking about real, strategic investing. It's one of the most effective ways to grow your wealth over time.

Investing is all about making your money work for you. You put your money into something like stocks, bonds, or real estate with the expectation that it will grow over time. It's like planting a money tree. It might take a while to bear fruit, but once it does, you'll be enjoying the sweet taste of financial success.

Now, there are many types of investments to consider. Stocks and bonds are the most common. When you buy a stock, you're buying a piece of a company. If the company does well, the price of the stock goes up and you make money. Bonds, on the other hand, are like loans. You lend money to a company or government, and they pay you back with interest.

Real estate is another popular investment. Whether it's buying a rental property or investing in a Real Estate Investment Trust (REIT), real estate can provide steady income and appreciation over time.

But here's the thing about investing: it's not a get-rich-quick scheme. It takes time and patience. And yes, there's risk involved. The value of your investments can go down as well as up. But with careful planning and diversification (that's investing in a variety of different things to spread the risk), you can manage that risk and grow your wealth.

So, stop letting your money sit idle in a savings account earning peanuts in interest. Start investing. Your future self will thank you.

Entrepreneurship

OK, let's talk about the big one: entrepreneurship. Now, I'm not going to sugar-coat it. Starting a business is tough. It's like climbing a mountain while juggling flaming swords. But when you reach the top, the view is unbeatable.

Entrepreneurship is the ultimate way to take control of your income. Instead of waiting for the payday, you're creating your own. You're the boss. You call the shots. It's scary, but it's also incredibly empowering.

Now, starting a business begins with an idea. Maybe you've found a way to solve a problem no one else is solving. Or maybe you have a product or service you're passionate about. Whatever it is, it has to be something people are willing to pay for. Otherwise, it's not a business, it's a hobby.

Once you have your idea, you need a plan. This is where a business plan comes in. It's like a roadmap for your business. It outlines what you're going to do and how you're going to do it. It's also crucial if you're planning to seek funding.

Speaking of funding, starting a business often requires some upfront investment. This could come from your savings, a bank loan, or investors. Just remember, borrowing money to start a business comes with risk. Make sure you understand what you're getting into.

And then there's the commitment. Running a business is often an uphill battle. It requires time, energy, and a whole lot of perseverance. There will be obstacles. There will be setbacks. But remember, every successful entrepreneur has faced failure. It's not about avoiding failure, it's about learning from it.

So, if you're ready to take control of your financial future, consider entrepreneurship. It's not for the faint of heart, but the rewards can be life-changing. The only limit to your income is your imagination and your willingness to act.

Leveraging Social Media and Online Platforms

Now it's time to talk about the elephant in the room: the internet. You know, that thing you spend hours on every day, scrolling through cat videos and arguing with strangers. What if I told you that you could be using it to make money? Mind-blowing, right?

In today's digital age, there are countless opportunities to monetize your online presence. You just need to know where to look and be willing to put yourself out there.

Let's start with social media. If you have a knack for creating engaging content and building a following, platforms like Instagram, YouTube, and TikTok can be gold mines. Whether it's through sponsored posts, ad revenue, or selling your own products or services, social media can be a lucrative side hustle or even a full-time gig.

For instance, if you're a food enthusiast, you could start an Instagram page or a YouTube channel where you share recipes, cooking tips, and food reviews. Once you've built a substantial following, food brands might pay you to feature their products in your posts or videos.

If you're into fashion, you could start a fashion blog or a TikTok account where you share fashion tips, outfit ideas, and product reviews. You could earn income through affiliate marketing, where you promote fashion products and earn a commission on any sales made through your referral link.

Or let's say you're really good at makeup. You could start a YouTube channel where you share makeup tutorials, review products, and share tips and tricks. Once you've built a substantial following, makeup brands might pay you to feature their products in your videos.

Online teaching and coaching have also become popular ways to earn income online. If you're knowledgeable in a certain area, you could create an online course or offer coaching sessions. Platforms like Teachable, Udemy, and Zoom make it easy to share your knowledge and skills with the world.

Or maybe you're a fitness enthusiast. You could create a fitness program and sell it on your own website or on a platform like Teachable. You could also offer personal training sessions over Zoom.

And let's not forget about blogging. If you love writing and have expertise in a certain area, starting a blog can be a great way to earn income through ad revenue, sponsored posts, and affiliate marketing.

The key to success online is providing value. Whether it's entertaining content, useful information, or a product or service that solves a problem, if you provide value, the money will follow.

So, stop wasting your time online and start making it work for you. With the right strategy and platform, the internet can be a gold mine.

Summary and Key Takeaways

Alright, we've covered a lot of ground here. From climbing the corporate ladder to starting your own business, from selling your old junk to investing in the stock market, there are countless ways to increase your income. But remember, it's not just about making more money. It's about what you do with that money that counts.

Here's the deal. Increasing your income is a crucial part of achieving financial freedom. But it's not a magic bullet. It's a tool. And like any tool, it's only as good as the person using it. You can have all the money in the world, but if you don't use it wisely, you'll end up right back where you started.

So, as you explore these strategies, keep your end goal in mind. Whether it's paying off debt, building an emergency fund, or investing for the future, any extra money you earn should be put to work towards that goal.

This isn't a get-rich-quick scheme. It's a get-rich-sure plan. It takes time, effort, and a whole lot of perseverance. But trust me, the journey is worth it. Because the destination is financial freedom.

Chapter 9

Reduce Expenses

You know that feeling when you see something you want, and you just have to have it? Maybe it's a shiny new phone, a fancy pair of shoes or the latest console game. You whip out your credit card, make the purchase, and for a moment, you feel good. But then the bill comes, and reality sets in. You've spent money you don't have on something you don't need. And now you're one step further from financial freedom.

Here's the hard truth: If you want to achieve financial freedom, you need to get your spending under control. You just need to spend less. And not just on the big things, like your house or your car, but on the little things too. Those fancy sunglasses, those impulse buys, they all add up.

We've discussed assessing your financial situation and budgeting at length in previous chapters so I won't make you go through that pain again. We're going straight into ways of reducing expenses in a manageable and sustainable manner.

Reducing Housing Costs

Let's tackle the big one first: housing. Whether you're renting or paying a mortgage, housing is likely your biggest expense. But just because it's a big expense doesn't mean it can't be reduced. It's time to get creative and think outside the box.

First, consider your living situation. Do you really need all that space? Could you get by in a smaller, cheaper place? Downsizing can save you a bundle, not just on rent or mortgage payments, but on utilities, maintenance, and other housing-related costs.

If downsizing isn't an option, consider refinancing your mortgage. Interest rates are not at their lowest at the moment but if you're on a very high rate, refinancing could significantly reduce your monthly payments. Just make sure you understand the costs involved and how they will impact your long-term financial goals.

Renting? Don't be afraid to negotiate. Many landlords would rather keep a good tenant at a lower rent than risk the place being empty or trashed by a careless new tenant. And if you're looking for a place, consider the location. Sometimes, moving a little further out can get you a lot more bang for your buck.

And then there's the nuclear option: getting a roommate. Yes, it might cramp your style, but splitting the rent and utilities can make a big dent in your expenses. If you have a spare room, you could also consider renting it out on Airbnb. Just make sure you understand the legal and tax implications.

Remember, your home is a place to live, not a status symbol. Don't let a fancy address or a big household you back from financial freedom. It's not about where you live; it's about how you live. And living debt-free is a lot more satisfying than any fancy house.

Saving on Transportation

Now let's talk about your wheels. That shiny piece of metal that gets you from point A to point B. It's convenient, it's comfortable, and it's costing you a fortune. Between the cost of the car itself, insurance, tax, fuel, maintenance, and parking, transportation is likely one of your biggest expenses. So how can you cut those costs?

First, consider your car situation. Do you really need a car? If you live in a city with good public transportation, you might be better off without one. Buses, trams, and trains can get you where you need to go for a fraction of the cost of owning a car.

If public transportation isn't an option, consider carpooling. Sharing the ride with others can save you a bundle on fuel and parking costs. Plus, it's better for the environment.

And then there's the car itself. If you're making payments on a new car, you're paying for more than just transportation.

You're paying for the privilege of driving a new car. Consider buying a used car instead. They're cheaper to buy, cheaper to insure, and often just as reliable as new cars.

If you need a car but don't use it often, consider renting or car sharing. Services like Zipcar let you rent a car by the hour, which can be much cheaper than owning a car you rarely use.

And don't forget about biking or walking. Not only are they free, but they're also great for your health.

A car is a tool, not a status symbol. Don't let a fancy car drive you into debt. It's not about what you drive; it's about where you're going. And where you're going is financial freedom.

Cutting Utility Bills

Alright, let's move on to utilities. You know, those pesky bills that show up every month for things like electricity, water, and heating. They're a necessary part of life, but that doesn't mean you can't cut them down to size.

First, let's talk about electricity. Are you leaving lights on in rooms you're not using? Are your electronics plugged in 24/7, sucking up power even when they're not in use? These little things add up. So, start turning off lights, unplug your electronics, and consider using energy-saving bulbs.

Next up, heating and cooling. Adjusting your thermostat by just a few degrees can save you a bundle. In the winter, put on a sweater instead of cranking up the heat. In the summer, use fans and close your blinds to keep your home cool.

Water is another area where you can save. Take shorter showers, fix leaky faucets, and don't run the dishwasher or washing machine until you have a full load.

And don't forget about energy-efficient appliances. They might cost more upfront, but they can save you money in the long run by using less power.

Utilities are a necessity, but wasting energy is not. By being mindful of your energy use, you can cut your utility bills and do your part for the environment. It's a win-win. So, start making these small changes, and watch your utility bills shrink.

Reducing Entertainment and Leisure Costs

Can we talk about fun now? Yes, even on a budget, you're allowed to have fun. But that doesn't mean you need to spend a fortune on entertainment and leisure activities. With a little creativity, you can have a great time without breaking the bank.

First, let's talk about those expensive hobbies. Whether it's golf, skiing, or collecting rare comic books, hobbies can be a major drain on your wallet. But they don't have to be. Look for cheaper alternatives or ways to cut costs. Maybe you buy used golf clubs instead of new ones, or you go skiing on weekdays when lift tickets are cheaper.

Next, let's talk about nights out. Going to the movies, concerts, or sporting events can be a lot of fun, but it can also be a lot of money. Look for discounts or cheaper alternatives. Maybe you have a movie night at home with friends, or you go to a local high school or college game instead of a pro game.

And don't forget about all the free or low-cost entertainment options out there. Parks, beaches, hiking trails, community events, public libraries, and museums often offer hours of entertainment for little or no cost.

Fun doesn't have to be expensive. It's not about how much you spend, it's about how much you enjoy. So, get creative, think outside the box, and start having fun on a budget.

Re-evaluating Insurance Policies

Insurance is one of those things you hate to pay for but are glad to have when you need it. But just because it's necessary doesn't mean you have to overpay for it.

- **Car insurance:** Are you paying for coverage you don't need? If your car is older and not worth much, you might be better off dropping collision and comprehensive coverage. And always shop around. Rates can vary widely from one company to another.

- **Home insurance:** Again, make sure you're not over-insured. You want enough coverage to rebuild your home and replace your belongings, but not more. Also, consider raising your deductible. A higher deductible will lower your premium, but make sure you have enough saved to cover it in case of a claim.

- **Life insurance:** If you have dependents, you need life insurance. But if you're single with no dependents, you might not need it at all. And if you do need it, term life insurance is usually a better deal than whole life.

Remember, insurance is about protecting against financial disaster, not against every little thing that could go wrong. So, review your policies, shop around, and make sure you're not paying more than you need to.

Trimming Debt and Bank Fees

First, let's talk about interest. It's the price you pay for borrowing money, and it can add up quickly. One way to reduce the amount of interest you pay is to consolidate your debt. This involves taking out a new loan to pay off your existing debts. The new loan should have a lower interest rate, which will save you money over time.

Refinancing is another option. This involves replacing your existing loan with a new one that has better terms, like a lower interest rate. This can save you money on your monthly payments and over the life of the loan.

Now, let's talk about bank fees. These are the little charges that banks love to tack onto your account. Overdraft fees, ATM fees, account maintenance fees, the list goes on. But here's the thing: many of these fees can be avoided. Keep track of your balance to avoid overdrafts, use your bank's ATMs to avoid ATM fees, and shop around for a bank that doesn't charge monthly fees.

Debt is a tool after all. Used wisely, it can help you achieve your financial goals. Used unwisely, it can keep you from them. So, be smart about your debt. Pay it down as quickly as possible, avoid unnecessary fees, and use it as a stepping stone to financial freedom.

Making Use of Technology

We live in a digital age, and technology can be a powerful tool for managing your finances and reducing your expenses. So, let's put that smartphone to work.

- **Budgeting apps:** These apps can help you track your income and expenses, set financial goals, and even alert you when you're about to overspend. Some popular options include Mint, YNAB (You Need A Budget), and PocketGuard. Find one that works for you and use it religiously.

- **Comparison shopping:** Why pay full price when you don't have to? Use price comparison websites to make sure you're getting the best deal. And don't forget about discount sites and apps. Sites like Groupon and RetailMeNot can save you a bundle on everything from dining out to home goods.

- **Online banking:** Most banks now offer online and mobile banking services. You can use these to keep track of your accounts, pay bills, transfer money, and even deposit checks. This can save you time and money on trips to the bank or ATM.

Used wisely, technology can help you save money and manage your finances more effectively. But like any tool, it's only as good as the person using it. So, use these apps and websites to your advantage, but don't let them replace good old-fashioned common sense and discipline.

Summary and Key Takeaways

From downsizing your home to cutting utility bills, from re-evaluating your insurance to avoiding bank fees, there are countless ways to reduce your expenses. But remember, it's not just about spending less. It's about spending smarter.

Here's the deal. Reducing your expenses is a crucial part of achieving financial freedom. But it's not a magic bullet. You can cut your expenses to the bone, but if you're not using the money you save wisely, you're just spinning your wheels.

So, as you explore these strategies, keep your end goal in mind. Whether it's paying off debt, building an emergency fund, or investing for the future, any money you save should be put to work towards that goal.

And remember, this isn't a one-time thing. Your life and your circumstances will change, and your spending should change with it. Regularly review your expenses and adjust as needed.

Chapter 10

Don't Go Overboard

So you're on a mission to cut costs and get out of debt, right? You're clipping coupons, skipping meals out, and you've even started considering whether you really need that Netflix subscription. But here's the thing: while it's great to be conscious of your spending, there's a line between being frugal and going overboard. And once you cross that line, you're not doing yourself any favours.

You see, there's a dangerous myth out there that the path to financial freedom is paved with extreme austerity; that if you just cut out all the fun and live like a monk, you'll be debt-free in no time. But let me tell you something, that's a one-way ticket to Burnout City. And once you're there, it's a lot harder to stay motivated and stick to your financial goals.

So, in this chapter, we're going to debunk that myth. We're going to talk about the dangers of going overboard in cost-cutting, and how to strike a balance between saving money and living a fulfilling life. Because, believe it or not, you can do both. And you don't have to sell your grandmother's antique brooch on eBay to do it. So, buckle up and let's get started.

Over-Austerity

It's a fancy term, but what does it really mean? Well, think of it like this: you're on a diet, but instead of cutting out junk food and eating more veggies, you decide to just stop eating altogether. That's over-austerity in a nutshell. It's like deciding to lose weight by starving yourself. It's the financial equivalent of a starvation diet, and let me tell you, it's just as painful and just as ineffective.

In the realm of personal finance, over-austerity is like going on a spending diet so extreme, that you're practically gnawing on the bones of your budget. It's about trying to pay off debt by cutting your spending down to the bare minimum. It's about saying no to everything, even the things you need or that bring you joy. It's about deprivation, not moderation. It's like trying to survive on water and air alone.

Now, don't get me wrong. When you're in debt, some degree of austerity is necessary. You need to cut back, live within your means, and prioritize your spending. It's like eating healthier and exercising more when you're trying to lose weight. But over-austerity is when you take this to an extreme. It's when you cut so much that it's not sustainable or healthy in the long term. It's like trying to run a marathon after fasting for a week.

Over-austerity can look like skipping meals to save on groceries, avoiding necessary medical care because of the cost, or never allowing yourself any leisure activities or treats. It's a life of constant self-denial and deprivation. It's like living in a world where all the colour has been drained out, and all that's left is a bleak, grey landscape of "no."

And here's the kicker: over-austerity doesn't even work in the long run. Just like a crash diet, it's not sustainable. You might save some money in the short term, but eventually, you'll burn out. You'll be so miserable and deprived that you'll end up splurging and undoing all your progress. It's like starving yourself for a week and then binging on a whole pizza and a tub of ice cream. So, while it might seem like a good idea on the surface, over-austerity is a trap that can keep you stuck in a cycle of debt and deprivation.

So, the next time you're thinking about going on a financial diet, remember: moderation, not deprivation. It's about making sustainable changes, not starving yourself. Because in the end, over-austerity is just a fancy term for a strategy that doesn't work.

The Dangers

You might think that cutting your spending to the bone is the fastest way to get out of debt, but it can actually backfire in a big way.

First off, over-austerity can lead to a serious dip in your quality of life. Imagine living in a world where you're constantly saying no to yourself, where every day is a struggle against deprivation. You're always stressed about money, always worried about spending, always feeling guilty about every little purchase. It's like living in a constant state of financial anxiety. That's no way to live, my friend.

Second, it can lead to burnout. Just like a car running on fumes, you can only keep going for so long before you break down. And when you're burned out, it's hard to stay motivated and stick to your debt repayment plan. It's like trying to run a marathon without any training. Sooner or later, you're going to hit a wall.

Third, over-austerity can lead to splurging. When you're constantly denying yourself, it's easy to swing to the other extreme and splurge on a big purchase. It's like starving yourself all day and then binging on junk food at night. It's not healthy, and it's not effective. It's like taking one step forward and two steps back.

And finally, over-austerity can keep you stuck in a scarcity mindset. When you're always focused on cutting costs and saving money, you can miss out on opportunities to increase your income and grow your wealth. Getting out of debt isn't just about spending less; it's also about earning more. It's like trying to fill a bucket with a hole in it. You can pour in as much water as you want, but if you don't fix the hole, you're never going to get anywhere.

So, while it might seem like a good idea to cut your spending to the bone when you're trying to repay debt, it's important to avoid the pitfalls of over-austerity. The goal isn't just to get out of debt; it's to build a better life for yourself. And that requires a balanced, sustainable approach to personal finance. It's about finding a middle ground, a place where you can live comfortably without living beyond your means. Because in the end, life is about more than just money. It's about happiness, fulfilment, and peace of mind. And those are things you can't put a price on.

Sustainable Spending

This is the sweet spot between overspending and over-austerity. It's about making smart, conscious decisions about how you use your money. It's about getting the most value for your money, without feeling deprived or stressed.

Sustainable spending is crucial when you're repaying debt. Why? Because it's sustainable. It's something you can keep up in the long term, without burning out or feeling miserable. And that's key to staying motivated and sticking to your debt repayment plan.

Maintaining necessary and beneficial spending is the essence of sustainable spending. This includes things like healthy food, necessary medical care, and activities that bring you joy and improve your quality of life. If your favourite series on Netflix serves as a stress relief, then don't cancel your subscription. It could do more harm than good. If you're spending four hours a day binge-watching it, however, you would probably be better off without it because you can use those four hours to make some money. So the goal isn't to live in deprivation; it's to live within your means.

Finally, sustainable spending means avoiding deprivation-induced splurging. When you're constantly denying yourself, it's easy to swing to the other extreme and make impulsive purchases. But when you're practising sustainable spending, you're less likely to feel deprived and more likely to make smart, conscious spending decisions.

At the end of the day, sustainable spending isn't about cutting costs at all costs. It's about making smart, conscious decisions about how you use your money. It's about getting the most bang for your buck, without feeling deprived or stressed. And that's a crucial part of repaying debt and achieving financial freedom.

Striking a Balance

You know, that elusive state where you're saving enough to pay off your debt, but not so much that you're living in a cardboard box. It's a tricky thing to achieve, but it's crucial if you want to repay your debt without losing your mind.

First off, let's be clear: saving for debt repayment is important. You need to be putting a significant chunk of your income towards your debt if you want to get rid of it. But that doesn't mean you should be living on noodles and tap water. You still need to maintain necessary and sustainable spending.

So, how do you strike this balance? It starts with mindful budgeting. You need to know where your money is going and make conscious decisions about how to spend it. This means prioritizing your spending based on your values and goals. It means spending on the things that truly matter to you and cutting back on the things that don't.

Setting realistic financial goals is also crucial. You need to have a clear idea of how much you need to save for debt repayment, and how much you can afford to spend on other things. If you don't know where you want to go, then it doesn't matter which way you're going right?

Finally, understand the difference between frugality and deprivation. Frugality is about making smart choices and getting the most value for your money. Deprivation is about cutting costs at all costs, even if it means sacrificing your quality of life. Aim for frugality, not deprivation.

Remember, striking a balance between saving for debt repayment and sustainable spending isn't easy. It requires discipline, mindfulness, and a willingness to make tough decisions. But it's crucial if you want to repay your debt without losing your mind. So, keep these strategies in mind, and start striking that balance today.

Spending For Growth

This is where you spend money on things that will help you increase your income, improve your skills, or enhance your well-being in the long run. You're investing in yourself and your future and believe it or not, it can actually help you repay your debt faster.

You see, when you're focused solely on cutting costs, it's easy to overlook the potential benefits of strategic spending. But the truth is, sometimes you have to spend money to make money. And that's where growth-oriented spending comes in.

For example, let's say you spend money on a course that helps you learn a new skill. This is an example of growth-oriented spending. Yes, it's an expense, but it's an expense that could lead to higher income in the future. It's an investment in yourself and your earning potential.

Or maybe you spend money on a gym membership to stay healthy. Again, this is an expense, but it's an expense that could save you money on medical bills in the future. It's an investment in your health and well-being.

The key here is to differentiate between mindless spending and strategic, growth-oriented spending. Mindless spending is when you spend money on things that don't bring you value or contribute to your goals. Growth-oriented spending, on the other hand, is when you spend money on things that will help you grow and achieve your goals.

So, as you work on repaying your debt, don't forget about the role of growth-oriented spending. Remember, it's not just about cutting costs; it's also about making smart, strategic investments in yourself and your future.

Summary and Key Takeaways

Alright, let's wrap this up. We've talked about the dangers of going overboard in cost-cutting, the importance of balanced spending, and the role of growth-oriented spending in debt repayment. So, what are the key takeaways?

First, avoid the trap of over-austerity. Cutting your spending to the bone might seem like a good idea when you're drowning in debt, but it can actually do more harm than good. It's like trying to lose weight by chopping off a leg. Sure, you'll be lighter, but you'll also be hopping around on one foot. Not exactly a sustainable solution, is it? So, be frugal, but don't be the guy who reuses his dental floss.

Second, practice sustainable spending like eating a balanced diet. You wouldn't survive on candy alone (as much as we'd all like to), and you can't manage your finances by cutting out all the good stuff. Make smart, conscious decisions about how you use your money. Prioritize your spending based on your values and goals. Maintain necessary and beneficial spending. And avoid deprivation-induced splurging.

Third, strike a balance between saving for debt repayment and sustainable spending. Use mindful budgeting, set realistic financial goals, and understand the difference between frugality and deprivation. This is not just about spending less; it's also about spending smarter. It's like walking a tightrope. Lean too far one way, and you're living in a cardboard box. Lean too far to the other, and you're buried under a mountain of debt. So, find your balance, and whatever you do, don't look down.

Finally, don't forget about growth-oriented spending. Invest in yourself and your future. Spend money on things that will help you increase your income, improve your skills, or enhance your well-being in the long run. Sometimes you have to spend money to make money. It's like planting a tree. You've got to water it, give it sunlight, and maybe even talk to it (hey, who am I to judge?). It might cost you a bit now, but in the future, you'll have a beautiful tree that's giving you shade, fruit, or maybe even money if you're into selling lumber.

So, there you have it. The path to financial freedom isn't about cutting costs at all costs. It's about making smart, conscious decisions about how you use your money. It's about getting the most value for your buck, without feeling deprived or stressed. And that's a crucial part of repaying debt and achieving financial freedom.

Chapter 11

Debt Snowball vs. Debt Avalanche

Alright, it's time to get down to the nitty-gritty. Choosing a debt repayment strategy is like choosing a workout plan. You wouldn't walk into a gym and just start lifting random weights, would you? No, you'd have a plan. You'd know which exercises to do, in what order, and how many reps to aim for. The same goes for repaying your debt. You need a plan, a strategy, and a method to the madness.

In this chapter, we're going to talk about two popular methods: the Debt Snowball and the Debt Avalanche. They might sound like something out of a disaster movie, but trust me; they're your ticket to a debt-free future. The only disaster here is not having a plan to tackle your debt. So, let's get to it!

Debt Snowball

Now, I guess I'm not wrong in assuming you've already pictured a snowball rolling down a hill. It starts small but as it rolls, it picks up more snow. It gets bigger and bigger, faster and faster, until it's a giant ball of unstoppable momentum. That's the Debt Snowball method in a nutshell.

Here's how it works: You start by focusing all your extra money on paying off your smallest debt first, while still making minimum payments on your other debts. Once that debt is paid off, you take the money you were throwing at that debt and roll it into the next smallest debt. You keep this up, tackling each debt in turn from smallest to largest.

Now, I know what you're thinking: "Vick, why on earth would I focus on the smallest debt? Shouldn't I be tackling the big ones first?" Well, that's where the psychology comes in. The Debt Snowball method is all about quick wins. You see, paying off a debt, no matter how small, feels good. It's a victory. It's a sign that you're making progress. And that feeling of progress is incredibly motivating.

Think about it. If you're trying to lose weight, and you lose a pound in your first week, you're going to feel good, right? You're going to feel motivated to keep going. The same principle applies to paying off debt. By starting with the smallest debt, you get to feel that rush of victory sooner. And that can give you the momentum you need to keep going.

But when is the Debt Snowball method ideal? Well, if you're the type of person who thrives on motivation, this could be the method for you. It's also a good choice if you have a lot of small debts that are causing you stress. Knocking those out quickly can give you a sense of control over your financial situation. It's like cleaning your house. You start with one room, then move on to the next, and before you know it, your whole house is clean.

Debt Avalanche

Now, let's shift gears and talk about the Debt Avalanche method. If the Debt Snowball method is all about momentum and motivation, the Debt Avalanche method is all about cold, hard math. It's the Spock to the Debt Snowball's Kirk, the Sherlock Holmes to its Dr. Watson. It's logical, it's efficient, and it's all about saving you money.

Here's how it works: Instead of starting with your smallest debt, like in the Debt Snowball method, you start with the debt that has the highest interest rate. You throw all your extra money into that debt while making minimum payments on your other debts. Once that high-interest debt is paid off, you move on to the debt with the next highest interest rate. You keep this up until all your debts are paid off.

This method is meant to save you the most money. You see, the higher the interest rate on a debt, the more it's costing you. By paying off your high-interest debts first, you reduce the total amount of interest you pay over time. It's like cutting off the head of the snake. Once you get rid of the debt with the highest interest, it's easier to tackle the rest.

But when is the Debt Avalanche method ideal? If you're a numbers person and you're focused on saving as much money as possible, this could be the method for you. It's also a good choice if you have one or two debts with significantly higher interest rates than your other debts.

However, the Debt Avalanche method requires discipline. It's like going on a diet. You can't just eat a salad one day and expect to lose weight. You have to stick with it. So, if you're ready to buckle down, make some sacrifices, and save some serious money, the Debt Avalanche method could be your ticket to a debt-free future.

Comparing Debt Snowball and Debt Avalanche

Alright, now that we've got a handle on both the Debt Snowball and Debt Avalanche methods, let's put them head to head. On one side, we've got the Debt Snowball for motivation and quick wins. On the other side, we've got the Debt Avalanche, the way for efficiency and interest savings. Which will come out on top? Well, that depends on you.

Let's imagine you have three debts: a £ 3,000 credit card debt with a 36% interest rate, a £ 1,500 personal loan with a 12% interest rate, and a £5,000 line of credit with an 8% interest rate.

If you use the Debt Snowball method, you'd start by paying off the £ 1,500 personal loan because it's the smallest. You'd feel a rush of victory as you eliminate that debt, and you'd roll that momentum into tackling the £ 3,000 credit card. Finally, you'd take on the £5,000 line of credit. You'd be riding high on a wave of quick wins, and that motivation could keep you going until you're debt-free.

If you use the Debt Avalanche method, you'd start with the £ 3,000 credit card debt because it has the highest interest rate. You'd be saving money right off the bat by reducing the amount of interest you're paying. Then, you'd move on to the £1,500 personal loan, and finally, you'd tackle the £5,000 line of credit. You'd be a lean, mean, interest-saving machine, and that could save you a lot of money in the long run.

Criteria	Snowball	Avalanche
Order of Repayment	Smallest to Largest Debt	Highest to Lowest Interest Rate
Psychological Benefit	High (quick wins)	Moderate (requires patience)
Interest Savings	Lower	Higher
Time to Debt Freedom	Depends on Debts	Often Faster
Best For	Those needing motivation	Those focused on saving money

Table. 7

When it comes to choosing between the Debt Snowball and Debt Avalanche methods, it's not about which method is objectively better. It's about which method is better for you. It's like choosing between a sports car and a minivan. If you're a single person who loves speed, the sports car is the better choice. But if you've got a family of five and a dog, the minivan is going to be a lot more practical.

The Debt Snowball method, with its focus on quick wins and motivation, might be the sports car of debt repayment methods. It's exciting, it's motivating, and it can get you where you're going fast… if where you're going is the land of debt freedom.

On the other hand, the Debt Avalanche method, with its focus on efficiency and interest savings, might be the minivan of debt repayment methods. It's practical, it's efficient, and it can save you a lot of money in the long run… if you're willing to stick with it.

So, take a good look at your debts, your personality, and your financial goals. Then, choose the method that's going to work best for you. And remember, the best debt repayment method is the one you stick with.

Assessing Your Debts

Now that we've got our methods down, it's time to take a good, hard look at your debts. I know, I know, it's about as fun as a root canal. But it's necessary. It's like going to the doctor. You might not want to hear that you need to lose weight or quit smoking, but you need that information to improve your health. The same goes for your financial health. You need to know the state of your debts to improve your financial situation.

So, how do you assess your debts? Well, it's not rocket science. You just need to gather some information. For each debt, you need to know the total amount you owe, the interest rate, and the minimum payment. This is the basic information you need to make an informed decision about which debt repayment method to use.

Think of it like a detective gathering clues. The total amount you owe is like the 'who' of your debt. It tells you which debts are the biggest and which are the smallest. The interest rate is like the 'what'. It tells you what each debt is costing you. The higher the interest rate, the more that debt is costing you. And the minimum payment is like the 'where'. It tells you where your money needs to go each month to keep up with your debts.

Once you've gathered all this information, you can start to see the big picture. You can see which debts are costing you the most and which are the smallest. You can see how much money you need to put towards your debts each month. And you can start to see which debt repayment method might work best for you.

So, grab a pen and paper, or open up a spreadsheet, and start assessing your debts. It might not be the most fun you've ever had, but it's an important step on your journey to debt freedom. And remember, knowledge is power. The more you

know about your debts, the better equipped you'll be to tackle t
hem.

Choosing Your Method

Alright, we've talked about the Debt Snowball method. We've talked about the Debt Avalanche method. Now, it's time to make a decision. It's like standing at a crossroads. You've got two paths in front of you, and you've got to choose which one to take.

Choosing a debt repayment method is a personal decision. It's like choosing a pair of shoes. You wouldn't buy a pair of shoes just because they look good on someone else, would you? No, you'd buy a pair of shoes because they fit you well and suit your style. The same goes for choosing a debt repayment method. You need to choose the method that fits your financial situation and suits your personality.

There are a few factors to consider when choosing a debt repayment method. First, consider your personal motivation. If you're the type of person who needs to see progress to stay motivated, the Debt Snowball method might be a good fit. It's all about quick wins and building momentum.

Second, consider the total amount of interest you'll pay. If you want to save as much money as possible, the Debt Avalanche method might be the way to go. It's all about efficiency and reducing the amount of interest you pay.

Third, consider your repayment timeline. If you want to get out of debt as quickly as possible, the Debt Avalanche method might be your best bet. But remember, it requires discipline and patience.

Finally, consider the importance of consistency and dedication. Whichever method you choose, you need to stick with it. It's like going on a diet. You can't just eat healthy for a week and expect to lose weight. You have to stick with it. The same goes for debt repayment. You need to stick with your chosen method and keep chipping away at your debt.

So, take some time to think about it. Weigh your options. Consider your financial situation, your personality, and your goals. Then, make your choice. And remember, there's no right or wrong choice. There's only the choice that's right for you. So, choose your path, take that first step, and let's start this journey to debt freedom together!

Complementing Your Chosen Method

So you've chosen your debt repayment method. You're either rolling up your debts like a snowball or you're causing an avalanche. Either way, you're taking action, and that's great. But let me tell you something. Paying off debt isn't just about throwing money at what you owe. It's like trying to lose weight by only exercising. Sure, you'll see some results, but if you're still eating junk food all day, you're not going to reach your goals.

So, what's the financial equivalent of eating junk food? Not budgeting and saving. If you're not keeping track of your money and setting some aside for the future, you're not going to reach your financial goals. It's as simple as that.

Budgeting is like a financial diet. It helps you keep track of what's coming in and what's going out. It helps you identify areas where you can cut back and areas where you might need to spend more. And most importantly, it helps you make sure that you're putting enough money towards your debts.

Saving, on the other hand, is like exercising. It helps you build up a financial buffer for the future. It gives you peace of mind knowing that you have money set aside for emergencies. And it helps you prepare for big expenses down the line.

So, how do you complement your chosen debt repayment method with budgeting and saving? Well, it's all about balance. You need to find a balance between paying off your debts, keeping up with your current expenses, and setting money aside for the future. It's like balancing on a tightrope. It might be tricky at first, but once you find your balance, you'll be able to walk across with confidence.

So, start by setting up a budget. Track your income and your expenses. See where your money is going and where you can cut back. Then, set up a savings plan. Decide how much you want to save each month and stick to it. And remember, every little bit helps. Even if you can only save a small amount each month, it's better than not saving at all.

Paying off debt is a marathon, not a sprint. It's going to take time and effort. But with the right method, a good budget, and a solid savings plan, you'll cross that finish line. So, lace up your shoes, get on that tightrope, and let's start this balancing act!

Modifying Your Method as Needed

Life, as you may know, is unpredictable. It's like a roller coaster. There are ups, there are downs, and sometimes there are loops that turn everything upside down. Your financial situation is no different. It can change, and when it does, your debt repayment method might need to change too.

Think of your debt repayment method as a road map. It's there to guide you, to show you the way. But what happens when there's a roadblock or a detour? Do you just give up and turn back? No, you find another way. You modify your route. The same goes for your debt repayment method.

Let's say you're using the Debt Snowball method. You're starting with your smallest debt and working your way up. But then, you get a big bonus at work. Suddenly, you have the means to pay off a large chunk of your most significant debt. In this case, it might make sense to switch to the Debt Avalanche method and use that bonus to tackle your highest-interest debt.

Or maybe you're using the Debt Avalanche method, but you're feeling overwhelmed. You're not seeing progress as quickly as you'd like, and it's starting to affect your motivation.

In this case, it might make sense to switch to the Debt Snowball method and give yourself a quick win to boost your morale.

The point is, that your debt repayment method isn't set in stone. It's a tool, and like any tool, it can be adjusted to fit your needs. So, don't be afraid to modify your method as needed. Just make sure that any changes you make are strategic and in line with your financial goals.

The goal isn't to stick to a specific method. The goal is to get out of debt. So, stay flexible, stay adaptable, and stay focused on your goal. You're not just a passenger on this roller coaster of life. You're the one in the driver's seat. So, hold on tight, keep your eyes on the road, and let's navigate this journey to debt freedom together!

Summary and Key Takeaways

Alright, we've covered a lot of ground in this chapter. We've talked about the Debt Snowball method and the Debt Avalanche method. We've discussed how to choose a method, how to complement it with budgeting and saving, and how to modify it as needed. It's been a wild ride, but we've made it to the end. So, let's take a moment to recap and reflect.

First and foremost, having a debt repayment strategy is crucial. It's like having a game plan in a football match. Without it, you're just running around the field, hoping to score a goal. But with it, you're working strategically towards victory. So, choose a method that suits your financial situation and your personality, and stick with it.

Second, your chosen method isn't the be-all and end-all. It's a tool, and like any tool, it needs to be used correctly. Complement your method with good financial habits, like budgeting and saving. And don't be afraid to modify your method as needed. Your financial situation can change, and your method should be able to change with it.

Finally, remember that the goal is to get out of debt. It's not about sticking to a specific method or following a particular set of rules. It's about improving your financial health and gaining freedom from your debts. So, keep your eyes on the prize, stay focused on your goal, and don't let anything distract you from it.

So, there you have it. That's the end of this chapter. But it's not the end of your journey. It's just the beginning. So, take what you've learned, apply it to your life, and start making progress towards debt freedom. And you're not alone in this. I'm here with you, cheering you on every step of the way. So, let's get out there and tackle that debt!

Chapter 12

Debt Consolidation & Refinancing Options

In the world of finance, there's no one-size-fits-all solution. Just as every individual is unique, so too are their financial circumstances. What works like a charm for one person might be a complete disaster for another. It's like trying to fit a square peg into a round hole - it's not just a poor fit, it's an impossible one. It just doesn't work.

That's why it's absolutely crucial to understand all the financial tools at your disposal. And two of the most potent tools you have at your disposal are debt consolidation and refinancing.

Now, I can almost hear the gears turning in your head. "Debt consolidation? Refinancing? Sounds like a complicated financial jargon." But don't let these terms intimidate you. It's not as scary as it sounds. In fact, these can be powerful strategies to manage and reduce your debt. But like any tool, they need to be used correctly and with precision. Misuse a hammer, and you're more likely to hit your thumb than the nail. So, let's dive in and learn how to wield these tools like a pro.

Debt Consolidation

Imagine this: You're standing in the middle of a room that's in complete disarray. There are piles of clothes, stacks of books, and a jumble of miscellaneous items scattered all over the place. It's overwhelming, right? Now, think of debt consolidation as the process of cleaning up this messy room.

Debt consolidation is like taking all your debts, which are currently scattered across various credit cards, loans, and lines of credit, all with different payment dates, and gathering them into one neat pile. It's about bringing order to the chaos. Instead of juggling multiple payments to multiple creditors each month, each with its own due date, interest rate, and balance, you're making one payment to one creditor. It's like cleaning up that messy room and putting everything in its rightful place.

But how does this work in practice? Well, there are several ways to consolidate your debt.

Consolidation Loan:

This is a type of loan that combines multiple debts into one single loan, typically with a lower interest rate and a longer repayment period.

- ***Advantages:*** The main advantage of a consolidation loan is that it simplifies your debt management. Instead of dealing with multiple creditors, you only have one loan to worry about. Additionally, the lower interest rate can save you a significant amount of money over the long term.

- ***Disadvantages:*** On the downside, consolidation loans can be tempting as they may free up additional credit, which can lead to further debt if not managed properly. Also, these loans often require good credit scores for approval, and they may also have upfront fees.

Balance Transfer Credit Card:

This involves transferring your credit card balances to a single card, usually with a lower introductory interest rate.

- ***Advantages:*** The primary advantage is the potential for significant interest savings, especially if you can pay off your balance during the low introductory rate period. It also simplifies your payments by consolidating multiple credit card debts into one.

- ***Disadvantages:*** Balance transfer cards often come with fees, typically a percentage of the transferred balance. Also, if you can't pay off the balance before the introductory rate expires, the remaining balance will be subject to a much higher interest rate. Like consolidation loans, this method also requires a good credit score.

Debt Management Program:

In this approach, a credit counselling agency negotiates with your creditors to reduce your interest rates and monthly payments.

- *Advantages:* These programs can provide relief by lowering your monthly payments and interest rates. They also offer the convenience of making a single monthly payment to the counselling agency, which then distributes the payments to your creditors.

- *Disadvantages:* Enrolling in a debt management program can impact your credit score. Additionally, these programs often require you to close your credit card accounts, which can be inconvenient. There may also be fees associated with the program.

So, as you can see, debt consolidation isn't just about simplifying your financial life. It's about making strategic decisions to manage your debt more effectively. It's about taking control of your financial situation and making it work for you, rather than against you. But like any financial strategy, it requires careful consideration and smart decision-making.

When to Use Debt Consolidation

So, you're probably wondering, "When is the right time to consider debt consolidation?" Well, the answer to that isn't as straightforward as you might think. It's not a one-size-fits-all kind of deal. It's more like choosing the perfect pair of shoes. You wouldn't wear high heels for a hiking trip, would you? Similarly, debt consolidation might be the perfect fit for one financial situation, but completely unsuitable for another.

Debt consolidation can be a great option if you're dealing with a significant amount of high-interest debt. If you're constantly juggling multiple credit card payments, for instance, consolidating these into one payment with a lower interest rate can save you a lot of money and stress.

But it's not just about the amount of debt or the interest rates. Your credit score plays a crucial role too. If you have a good credit score, you're more likely to qualify for a consolidation loan or balance transfer card with a lower interest rate.

And let's not forget about self-discipline. Debt consolidation can simplify your payments, but it won't stop you from accumulating more debt. That part is up to you. It's like getting a bigger closet to organize your clothes. It might help you keep your wardrobe tidy, but it won't stop you from buying more clothes than you need.

However, if you're struggling with secured debts like your mortgage or student loans, other options might be more suitable. Debt consolidation is generally more beneficial for unsecured debts like credit cards or personal loans.

So, when considering debt consolidation, it's essential to take a step back and assess your financial situation. Look at your debts, your interest rates, your credit score, and most importantly, your spending habits. Debt consolidation can be a powerful tool, but only if it's used in the right circumstances and with the right mindset.

Financial decisions are like footwear. You need to find the right fit for your situation. And sometimes, that means trying on a few different options before you find the perfect match. So, don't rush. Take your time, do your research, and make the decision that's best for you.

Refinancing

Now that we've tidied up our understanding of debt consolidation, let's shift our focus to another powerful financial tool: refinancing. If we continue with our earlier analogy, where debt consolidation was like cleaning up a messy room, then refinancing is like a full-scale home renovation. You're not just organizing your debt; you're fundamentally changing the terms of it.

Refinancing is like taking your old, worn-out loan and giving it a complete makeover. It's like swapping your old windows for new, energy-efficient ones. You're getting a new loan with better terms to replace your old loan. It's a chance to negotiate a lower interest rate, reduce your monthly payment, or even shorten the term of your loan.

Common types of debt that people often refinance include mortgages, student loans, and car loans. But why would you want to refinance these loans? Well, let's say you're a few years into your mortgage and interest rates have dropped significantly. By refinancing, you could potentially save thousands over the life of your loan. Or perhaps you've significantly improved your credit score since you took out your loans. Refinancing could help you secure a lower interest rate, reducing the overall amount you'll pay back.

But refinancing comes with its own set of considerations. On the upside, you could save a lot of money in the long run. On the downside, you might have to pay closing costs or extend the life of your loan.

So, as you can see, refinancing isn't a decision to be taken lightly. It requires a careful evaluation of your current financial situation, your future financial goals, and the current state of the lending market. But don't worry, we'll delve deeper into when and how to use refinancing, the potential pitfalls to avoid, and how to choose a lender in the following sections.

When to Use Refinancing

So, when is the right time to pull the trigger on refinancing? Well, much like our earlier discussion on debt consolidation, it's not a simple cut-and-dry answer. It's all about timing and circumstances. It's like deciding when to sell your house. You need to consider the market conditions, the value of your house, and your future plans.

In the case of refinancing, you need to consider several factors. First, take a look at the interest rates. If the rates have dropped significantly since you took out your original loan, it might be a good time to refinance. This is because a lower interest rate can reduce your monthly payments and the total amount you pay over the life of the loan.

Next, consider the length of your loan. If you're financially stable and can afford higher monthly payments, you might consider refinancing to a shorter-term loan. This can lead to substantial savings in interest over the life of the loan, much like an intense workout regimen can help you achieve your fitness goals faster. However, it's important to ensure that the higher payments won't strain your budget.

Don't forget about the closing costs. Refinancing isn't free. There are closing costs involved, which can include application fees, origination fees, appraisal fees, and others. These costs can add up, so it's essential to calculate whether the savings from a lower interest rate will outweigh these expenses. If the costs of refinancing are higher than the savings, it might not be the best move.

Your credit score is another factor to consider. If your score has improved since you took out your original loan, you might qualify for a better interest rate on a new loan. This is because lenders often offer better terms to borrowers with higher credit scores.

Lastly, your personal financial situation and future plans should be considered. If you plan to move or sell your house in the near future, for example, refinancing might not make sense as you may not recoup the costs before selling.

Remember, financial decisions are like a journey. You need to find the right path for your situation. Sometimes, that means exploring a few different routes before you find the perfect one. So, take your time, do your research, and make the decision that's best for you.

Potential Pitfalls of Debt Consolidation & Refinancing

As we journey through the landscape of debt consolidation and refinancing, it's important to be aware of the potential pitfalls that lie ahead. These strategies, while powerful, are not without their risks. It's like using a chainsaw. In the right hands, it can be an incredibly useful tool, helping you cut down a tree with ease. But if you don't know what you're doing, you could end up causing a lot of damage.

With debt consolidation and refinancing, there are several risks to be aware of. One of the most common pitfalls is the temptation to extend the term of your loan. While this might lower your monthly payments, it could end up costing you more in interest over the long run.

Another potential pitfall is ending up with a higher interest rate. This can happen if you consolidate or refinance without carefully shopping around for the best rates. It's like buying a car without comparing prices at different dealerships. You might end up paying more than you need to.

Then there's the impact on your credit score. Applying for a new loan or credit card (which you might do when consolidating or refinancing) can result in a hard inquiry on your credit report, which might lower your score.

And let's not forget the emotional and psychological aspects. Debt consolidation and refinancing can provide a sense of immediate relief, but they don't address the root cause of the debt. If you don't change your spending habits, you could end up in a cycle of recurring debt. It's like going on a crash diet. You might lose weight quickly, but you're likely to gain it all back if you don't change your eating habits.

So, as you can see, while debt consolidation and refinancing can be powerful tools in your financial toolbox, they need to be used wisely.

How to Choose a Debt Consolidation or Refinancing Provider

Choosing a debt consolidation or refinancing provider is a decision that requires careful thought and thorough research. It's like choosing a doctor or a mechanic. You wouldn't just go with the first one you find in the phone book or online. You need to dig a little deeper, compare their credentials, read reviews, and evaluate their rates.

In the world of debt consolidation and refinancing, there are several key factors to consider. First, look at the fees. Some providers might offer low-interest rates but make up for it with high fees. It's like choosing a budget airline. The ticket might be cheap, but you could end up paying a lot for baggage and other extras.

Next, be wary of unrealistic promises. If a provider promises to wipe out your debt or drastically lower your interest rate without knowing your financial situation, be cautious.

Also, watch out for pressure to make a quick decision. A reputable provider will give you time to consider your options and make an informed decision.

And let's not forget about predatory lenders. These are the sharks of the financial world. They prey on people in desperate situations, offering quick solutions that often lead to more problems.

So, how do you avoid these sharks? By shopping around and comparing rates. In the UK, you might consider providers like Zopa or Barclays for debt consolidation loans, while in the US, providers like SoFi or Discover could be options. For refinancing, UK residents might look at providers like HSBC or NatWest, and in the US, providers like Quicken Loans or Wells Fargo could be considered. Remember, these are just examples and it's important to do your own research to find the best fit for your situation.

Also, don't forget to ask questions and read the fine print. Understand the terms and conditions before you sign anything. It's like reading the contract before buying a house. You need to know what you're getting into.

And finally, trust your gut. If something sounds too good to be true, it probably is. It's like buying a used car. If the price is surprisingly low, there might be something wrong under the hood.

Choosing a debt consolidation or refinancing provider is a crucial step in your financial journey. It's not a decision to be taken lightly. So, take your time, do your research, and make the decision that's best for you

Summary and Key Takeaways

Well, we've travelled quite a distance together in this chapter. We've navigated the winding roads of debt consolidation and refinancing, explored the various routes they offer, and learned how to steer clear of potential pitfalls. But as we reach the end of this chapter, it's important to take a moment to reflect on our journey and remember the key takeaways.

Here are some key differences between debt consolidation and refinancing:

	Debt Consolidation	Refinancing
Purpose	Combine multiple debts into one	Replace one loan with another
Benefits	Simplify repayment, potentially lower interest rate	Potentially lower interest rate, better loan terms
Drawbacks	May extend repayment period, could result in higher total interest paid if not managed properly	May extend repayment period, could result in higher total interest paid if not managed properly

Table 8

First and foremost, remember that debt consolidation and refinancing are tools in your financial toolbox. They're not cure-all solutions or magic wands that will make your debt disappear in a puff of smoke. They're like a satnav on a road trip. It can guide you and help you navigate, but it won't drive the car for you.

Debt consolidation and refinancing can help you simplify your payments, lower your interest rate, or reduce your monthly payment. But they won't eliminate your debt. That part is up to you. Only you can do that, by making consistent payments, reducing your expenses, and increasing your income.

So, take what you've learned in this chapter and apply it to your situation. Consider your options, do your research, and make an informed decision.

And remember, you're not alone in this journey. I'm here with you, cheering you on every step of the way. It's like having a co-driver on a road trip. I'm here to help you navigate, keep you company, and celebrate with you when we reach our destination.

Chapter 13

Dealing with Debt Collectors

Ah, debt collectors. Those relentless, pesky gnats buzzing around your wallet, turning your peaceful financial picnic into a scene from "Jaws". But don't start running for the hills just yet. This chapter is your survival guide.

Dealing with debt collectors can feel like getting a root canal without anaesthesia. It's a reality many of us face when we're in debt, a reality that can feel about as pleasant as stepping barefoot on a Lego. But here's the deal: if you want to make it out in one piece, you've got to know the rules of the game.

This chapter is your secret weapon, your cheat sheet, your backstage pass to handling debt collectors like a pro. We're going to pull back the curtain on debt collection, exposing the grimy underbelly of this financial beast. We'll navigate the minefield, dodge the traps, and show you how to come out the other side with your sanity (and your credit score) intact.

So buckle up, put on your game face, and let's dive in headfirst.

Understanding Debt Collection

Debt collection. It's a phrase that can send shivers down the spine of even the toughest among us. It's like the bogeyman of the financial world, lurking in the shadows, ready to pounce when you least expect it. But let's pull back the curtain on this financial Frankenstein, shall we?

Debt collection is a practice as old as the concept of debt itself. It's a process that's been around since the dawn of civilization, when one caveman might have loaned another a few rocks and expected them back. Today, if you borrow money and don't repay it on time, the person or company you owe can hire a debt collector to recover that money.

These debt collectors are like the bounty hunters of the financial world, their quarry being your unpaid debt. Their sole mission is to recover what's owed. They can be independent agencies or part of the original company you owe. They earn their keep by getting you to pay up. Often, they buy your debt from the original creditor for a fraction of the amount and then try to collect the full amount from you. It's like buying a used car for a steal and then selling it for full price. It's not the most glamorous job, but someone's got to do it, right?

But here's where you need to be careful: not all of these financial predators play by the rules. They might try to intimidate you, harass you, or even mislead you about what you owe. But don't let them scare you. This is your financial future we're talking about here.

Remember, you have rights. You don't have to be subjected to intimidation or harassment. And you certainly shouldn't be misled about the amount you owe. Don't let the fear of debt collectors dictate your financial future. Stand your ground, know your rights, and strive for a fair resolution.

Knowing Your Rights

When it comes to dealing with debt collectors, you've got to know your rights. In the UK, these rights are primarily protected by the Consumer Credit Act. This legislation serves as a bulwark against aggressive debt collection tactics, outlining what debt collectors can and cannot do, and providing you with ways to safeguard yourself from their sometimes unscrupulous methods.

In the United States, a similar law exists known as the Fair Debt Collection Practices Act (FDCPA). It functions in much the same way, acting as a financial bodyguard for those dealing with debt collectors. However, for the purpose of this discussion, let's focus on the UK's Consumer Credit Act.

The Consumer Credit Act places restrictions on when and how frequently debt collectors can contact you. It also regulates what they can say and what actions they can take in their efforts to collect the debt. For instance, they cannot harass you, lie to you, or use unfair practices. They also cannot contact you at inconvenient times or places, such as before 8 a.m. or after 9 p.m., unless you agree to it.

Moreover, the Act gives you the right to dispute the debt if you believe it's not yours, it's been paid, or the amount is incorrect. You can request the debt collector to provide a detailed account of the debt, and they must cease collection activities until they've provided this information.

The Act also limits how your debts can be shared with others. Debt collectors cannot discuss your debt with anyone else without your permission, protecting your privacy. They also cannot publicly list your debt, or threaten to do so, as a method of forcing you to pay.

So, if a debt collector starts behaving like a rowdy football fan after a loss, you can use the provisions of the Consumer Credit Act to hold them accountable. You have the right to be treated fairly and respectfully, even when dealing with debt. Don't hesitate to seek legal advice if you feel a debt collector is violating your rights under the Consumer Credit Act.

But here's the kicker: These rights are as useful as a chocolate teapot if you don't know about them. So, consider this your call to arms. It's time to get educated, to arm yourself with knowledge, and to stand up for your rights.

Communication

Dealing with debt collectors can feel like you're walking a tightrope. It's a bit like playing a high-stakes poker game, where you've got to keep your cards - or in this case, your personal information and strategy - close to your chest. You can't afford to show all your cards at once, because that might give them an advantage.

Being firm and clear is key. You need to be assertive, but not aggressive. It's like being a quarterback in a football game - you need to be decisive and direct, but also keep your cool. And just like a quarterback keeps track of every play, you need to keep detailed records of all your interactions with the debt collectors. This includes dates, times, names, and the content of your conversations.

Staying calm is also crucial. Debt collectors can be as persistent as a seagull swooping down on a fish and chips stand, but you can't let them ruffle your feathers. Their job is to get you to pay, and they'll use all sorts of tactics to achieve that. But you're not a fish to be picked at; you're a person who deserves respect and fair treatment.

One strategy you can use is to request that debt collectors only contact you in writing. This gives you a paper trail, which can be a lifesaver if there are any misunderstandings or disputes. It's like having a referee in a boxing match - someone to ensure that the rules are followed and everything is above board. If a debt collector has made a mistake or confused you with someone else, this written communication can be your knockout punch to clear things up.

I know, I know, talking to debt collectors is probably the last thing you want to do. It's like being told you have to clean the gutters on a rainy day. But trust me, it's necessary and can save you a lot of headaches in the long run. So, put on your game face, take a deep breath, and tackle it head-on. You're not just a number in their ledger; you're a person with rights. And with the right knowledge and strategy, you can defend those rights like a pro.

Debt Validation

Alright, it's time to let you in on a little secret. It's called debt validation, and it's like the golden ticket in the world of debt collection. It's your secret weapon, your ace in the hole, your "Get Out of Jail Free" card.

Debt validation is a critical process when dealing with debt collectors. It's a bit like a reality check for them. Think of it this way: Imagine a door-to-door salesman shows up at your house, trying to sell you a vacuum cleaner. They claim it can suck up every speck of dust in your house. Now, you wouldn't just take their word for it, would you? You'd want them to prove it, to show you that the vacuum cleaner really does what they say it does.

That's exactly what debt validation is. It's your way of saying to the debt collector, "Prove it. Show me that I really owe this debt." If they can't provide this proof, they can't collect the debt. It's as simple and as powerful as that. It's like having a magic shield that can stop a debt collector in their tracks.

Now, how do you go about requesting debt validation? Well, you need to send a written request to the debt collector within 30 days of their initial contact. It's like hitting the pause button on a game console. The game - or in this case, the debt collection - can't proceed until they've responded to your request.

Once they receive your letter, they're obligated to stop all collection activities until they can provide concrete proof of the debt. This includes phone calls, letters, reporting the debt to credit bureaus, or any other collection activity. It's like putting them in a time-out until they can show you the evidence you've asked for.

And here's the thing: debt validation isn't just a right that you have; it's a power move. It's your way of saying, "I'm not just going to take your word for it. Show me the evidence." It's like being a detective in a crime drama, demanding to see the proof before making any conclusions.

By requesting debt validation, you're taking control of the situation. You're not just passively accepting what the debt collector says. Instead, you're actively challenging them, turning the tables on them. It's like being in a chess game where you suddenly put your opponent in check. They have to respond, and until they do, you've got the upper hand.

So, if you're dealing with debt collectors, don't forget about debt validation. It's not just a defensive move, it's an offensive one. It's a way of asserting your rights, of taking control, and of making sure that you're not being taken advantage of. It's a powerful tool and one that you should definitely use if you find yourself in this situation.

Negotiating

Negotiating with debt collectors can feel like you're playing a high-stakes game of chess, where every move you make can significantly impact the outcome. The goal here isn't to outwit or trick the collector but to get them to accept less than what you owe or to agree to a payment plan that fits within your budget. It's about clear, assertive communication and a thorough understanding of your financial situation. It's a bit like convincing a hungry lion that a salad is just as satisfying as a steak. It's not easy, but with the right strategy, it's possible.

Let's break it down a bit. The first step in this chess game is to understand your position on the board. You need to know exactly how much you owe and how much you can realistically afford to pay. This isn't the time for wishful thinking or empty promises. It's better to commit to a smaller amount that you can definitely pay than to agree to a larger sum and risk defaulting. It's like choosing to move a pawn forward instead of risking your queen in a risky play.

When you're in the throes of negotiation, it's crucial to stay calm and firm. Debt collectors might try to pressure or intimidate you into agreeing to terms that aren't in your best interest. They might try to corner your king, so to speak. But don't let them. Stand your ground and don't be afraid to push back. You're not just a pawn in their game; you're a player with rights and the power to negotiate.

And here's the golden rule, the checkmate move if you will: always, always, always get any agreement in writing. This is your proof, your safety net, and your insurance policy against any future disputes. It's like having a video replay of a sports game - it's undeniable proof of what happened. They always seem to lose phone recordings that don't play in their favour. So, don't just take their word for it. Get it in black and white.

Think of it this way: If you were buying a car, you wouldn't just shake hands and drive off. You'd want a contract, a written agreement that outlines the terms of the deal. The same principle applies when negotiating with debt collectors. It's not just a good idea; it's a necessity.

So, when you're negotiating with debt collectors, it's not about sweet-talking or trickery. It's about clear, assertive communication, a good understanding of your financial situation, and always getting agreements in writing. It's a delicate process, a high-stakes game of chess, but with the right moves, you can come out on top.

Debt Settlement

Debt settlement is a process where you negotiate with your creditors to pay a lump sum that is less than the full amount you owe. It's a tough negotiation, but if successful, it can significantly reduce your financial burden.

Now, let's be clear: debt settlement isn't a magic bullet. It can severely damage your credit score, and there's no guarantee your creditors will agree to a settlement. Plus, if you work with a debt settlement company, they'll likely charge you a fee for their services. So, it's essential to weigh the pros and cons before deciding on this route.

If you're considering debt settlement, do your homework. Research potential debt settlement companies, compare their fees and services, and check their reputation. Don't just go with the first company you find. Take your time, compare your options, and choose a company that offers the best balance of cost and service.

Also, remember that everything in debt settlement is negotiable, including the fees of the debt settlement company. Don't be afraid to haggle and push for the best possible terms. After all, this is your financial future we're talking about.

Finally, and I can't stress this enough, always get agreement in writing. Can you imagine a legal dispute where you know they're bending the truth but you don't have the evidence to prove it? I rest my case.

Debt settlement isn't easy, but with the right approach, it's manageable. And remember, you're not alone in this. With the right help and a bit of determination, you can navigate the process and come out on top.

Legal Action

This is the elephant in the room. It's the thing that everyone is most scared of when dealing with debt collectors. But that's mainly because most people don't know how to deal with it. With the right approach, you can weather this storm.

If a debt collector decides to sue you, it's like being called into the principal's office. It's serious, but it's not the end of the world. The first step is to respond. Ignoring it is like ignoring a leaking roof; it won't fix the problem and will only lead to more damage down the line. If you ignore the claim, the court will likely rule in favour of the debt collector by default.

The potential consequences of legal action can be severe. You could face wage garnishment, property liens, and other unpleasant outcomes. But remember, you have rights and options. It's like being stuck in a maze; there's always a way out, you just need to find it.

Here's a practical tip: If you're facing legal action, seek professional help. This could be a lawyer or a legal aid service. They can help you understand the claim, guide you through the process, and represent your interests in court. It's like having a seasoned guide when you're navigating a dense forest; they know the way and can help you avoid the pitfalls.

Also, remember that even at this stage, negotiation is still an option. You can negotiate with the debt collector, dispute the debt, or even file for bankruptcy in some cases. It's like being cornered in a boxing match; you still have moves you can make, you just need to choose the right one.

So, face up to legal action, if it comes to it, with courage and determination. It's a tough battle, but with the right help and a solid strategy, you can fight your way through.

Impact on Your Credit Score

When dealing with debt collectors, it can feel like your credit score is under siege. Every missed payment, every collection account, and every judgment against you can knock your score down a few pegs. It's like a financial game of Jenga; each move can make your credit score wobble a bit more.

But here's the good news: your credit score isn't set in stone. It's a fluid number that changes based on your financial behaviour. So, even if your score takes a hit, there are strategies for repairing your credit after dealing with debt collections.

You can start by getting a copy of your credit report. This is like getting a map of the battlefield; it shows you where the damage is and helps you plan your strategy. Look for any errors on your report, as these can unfairly drag down your score.

Next, focus on paying off your debts and maintaining good financial habits. This includes paying all your bills on time, keeping your credit card balances low, and not taking on new debt. It's like following a fitness regimen; it takes time and discipline, but the results are worth it.

Finally, keep an eye on your credit report. Monitor it regularly to track your progress and catch any errors or signs of identity theft. It's like keeping a health diary; it helps you track your progress and spot any potential problems early.

Summary and Key Takeaways

We've been through the wringer in this chapter, haven't we? We've navigated the treacherous waters of debt collection, climbed the mountain of negotiation, and braved the storm of legal action. We've faced down the beast of our credit score and emerged stronger and wiser. But before we close this chapter, let's take a moment to reflect on what we've learned.

Dealing with debt collectors is a challenge, but it's not an insurmountable one. It's like running a marathon; it's tough, it's gruelling, but with the right training and determination, you can cross the finish line.

Debt collectors are just normal people doing their job. They're not the enemy, but they're not your friend either. They're like the opposing team in a football match; you respect them, but you're not going to let them score without a fight.

Your job is to protect your rights, advocate for yourself, and work towards resolving your debts. It's like being a one-person army, defending your financial fortress from the onslaught of debt collectors. It's a tough job, but with the knowledge and tools you've gained from this chapter, you're more than up to the task.

This isn't just about surviving; it's about thriving. It's about taking control of your financial future, standing up for your rights, and working towards a debt-free life.

Chapter 14

Build an Emergency Fund

Now it's time to talk about something that's as exciting as watching paint dry but as necessary as a parachute when you're skydiving: the emergency fund. Now, I know what you're thinking. "Mate, I'm already knee-deep in debt, I'm trying to cut back on my triple-shot lattes, and now you want me to save money for a rainy day? Are you out of your mind?" Well, my friend, I might be a little crazy, but when it comes to financial health, an emergency fund is as sane as it gets.

In the simplest terms, an emergency fund is a stash of money you've set aside to cover those unexpected expenses that life loves to throw at you. It's like having a financial first aid kit. You hope you never have to use it, but when an emergency strikes, you'll be glad it's there.

You see, life has a funny way of throwing curveballs at us when we least expect it. One day you're cruising along, and the next, your car decides to give up the ghost or your boss hands you a P45 instead of a payslip. These are the moments when you'll be thanking your lucky stars (and me, of course) that you have an emergency fund.

An emergency fund is like the spare wheel for your car. It's not sexy, and it's not something you think about when everything's going smoothly. But when you hit a pothole and get a flat, that spare is going to be your best friend.

So, in a nutshell, an emergency fund is your financial safety net, your buffer against life's surprises, and your ticket to peace of mind. It's not a luxury; it's a necessity. And in the following sections, we're going to delve into how you can build one, even if you think you can't afford to. So, keep calm and carry on reading!

Why the Emergency Fund?

Now let's cut to the chase. An emergency fund isn't just a nice-to-have; it's a must-have. Why? Because life is unpredictable, and your finances need to be prepared for that unpredictability.

Think of your emergency fund as your financial bodyguard. It's there to protect you from the unexpected financial punches that life can throw. Got a leaky roof? Your emergency fund has got it covered. Car broke down? Your emergency fund steps in. Lost your job? Your emergency fund gives you a buffer while you find a new one.

Without an emergency fund, these unexpected expenses can force you into debt or cause you to make financial sacrifices in other areas (as if you were not doing enough of that already). You might have to use credit cards or loans to cover the costs, which can lead to a cycle of debt that's hard to break free from.

With an emergency fund, you have a buffer. You have time. You have options. You can cover the costs without going into debt or disrupting your budget.

And let's not forget the peace of mind it brings. Knowing you have a financial safety net can significantly reduce financial stress. You can sleep a little easier knowing you're prepared for whatever comes your way.

So, the bottom line is this: an emergency fund is a crucial part of your financial health. It's your protection against the unexpected. It's your financial bodyguard. And trust me; you want this bodyguard by your side.

How Much Should Be in?

So, how much should you have in your emergency fund? Well, the answer to that is as varied as the British weather. It depends on your personal circumstances, but a good rule of thumb, as suggested by most financial experts, is to aim for three to six months' worth of living expenses.

Now, I can hear you gasping, "Three to six months? Are you off your rocker?" But stay with me here because I don't mean three to six times what you earn now and I'm not talking about having a pile of cash to swim in. I mean having just enough to cover your essential expenses like rent or mortgage, utilities, food, and transport for a few months if your income takes a hit.

Here's how to figure it out:

- ***Calculate Your Monthly Expenses:*** Start by figuring out how much you spend each month. And I'm not just talking about the big stuff like rent and bills. Include everything from your Netflix subscription to your cheeky Nando's.

- ***Identify Essential Expenses:*** Next, identify which of these are essential expenses; the ones you absolutely must pay each month. This might include your rent or mortgage, utilities, groceries, car payments, and any debt repayments.

- ***Multiply by Three (or Six):*** Once you've got your total monthly essential expenses, multiply that number by three. That's the minimum amount you should aim to have in your emergency fund. If you want to be extra cautious, multiply it by six.

But remember, this is a goal, not a requirement. If the final number seems daunting, don't panic. The important thing is to start saving what you can now and gradually build up your emergency fund over time. Even a small emergency fund can make a big difference when unexpected expenses come up.

And one more thing: your emergency fund should be easily accessible, like in a savings account. This isn't money you're investing or locking away. It's money you might need at a moment's notice, so you want to be able to get to it quickly and without penalty.

So, there you have it. That's how you figure out how much should be in your emergency fund. It might seem like a big goal, but remember, every little helps. Start where you are, save what you can, and before you know it, you'll have a financial safety net ready to catch you when life throws a curveball.

How to Build it:

Alright, so you've got your target for your emergency fund. Now, how do you actually get there? Here are some strategies to help you build your emergency fund:

Set a Monthly Savings Goal: Start by setting a realistic monthly savings goal. This could be a set amount of money or a percentage of your income. The key here is consistency. Even if you can only afford to save a small amount each month, it will add up over time. I personally know people who started by saving £5 or £10 a month and it worked because that gave them confidence they could save and soon they were saving a lot more.

Automate Your Savings: One of the easiest ways to save is to automate it. Set up a direct debit to transfer money from your current account to your savings account each month. Do this right after you get paid, so you won't even miss the money. That's how you pay your taxes after all and I don't think you get to miss that payment.

Use Windfalls Wisely: Got a tax refund? A bonus at work? A generous birthday gift? Instead of blowing it on a shopping spree, put at least a portion of it into your emergency fund. You could split that into three parts. Put a third towards the debt you're now focused on, one-third in your emergency fund and the rest to treat yourself.

Save Your Change: This might sound old school, but it works. At the end of each day, put your loose change in a jar. Once the jar is full, deposit it into your emergency fund. Now I understand that very few people are still using cash, but for those who do, it works.

Use a Savings App: There are plenty of apps out there that can help you save. Some round up your purchases to the nearest pound and put the difference into savings. Others analyse your spending and automatically transfer money into savings when you can afford it. New ones are being created almost every day and the old ones are being upgraded. So there's a universe of apps for you to choose from.

All in all building an emergency fund is a boring but absolutely necessary part of your debt repayment plan. It might take some time to reach your goal, and that's okay. The important thing is to start saving now and keep at it. Before you know it, you'll have a fully stocked emergency fund ready to protect you from life's financial surprises. And trust me, that's a feeling worth saving for.

Maintaining and Using Your Emergency Fund

So, you've built up your emergency fund. Give yourself a pat on the back. But don't pop the champagne just yet. Building the fund is only half the battle. Now, you've got to maintain it and know when to use it.

If you dip into your emergency fund, make it a priority to replenish it. You never know when the next emergency will hit, so it's important to get your fund back up to its target level as soon as you can.

Your emergency fund isn't a set-it-and-forget-it thing. As your life changes, so should your emergency fund. If your expenses increase, your emergency fund should increase too. Review it at least once a year, or whenever you have a major life change like a new job or new family member.

Now, one thing you'll need to keep in mind is that your emergency fund is for emergencies. Not for holidays. Not for a new TV. Emergencies. If you're tempted to use it for non-emergencies, remind yourself of why you created it in the first place, how long it took to create, and how long it will take to replenish. And what if the proverbial hits the fan right after you've spent your emergency fund on a telly?

If you do have an emergency, however, don't feel guilty about using your emergency fund. That's what it's there for. Yes, it can be hard to see that balance go down, but remember, it's much better than going into debt.

Your emergency fund should be easily accessible, but not too accessible. It should be in a separate account from your regular current account to avoid temptation. But you should be able to get to it quickly if you need it.

Remember, your emergency fund is a safety net. It's there to catch you when life throws you a curveball. So, maintain it, use it wisely, and let it give you the peace of mind you need. Because let's face it, life is a lot more enjoyable when you're not constantly worrying about money.

Summary and Key Takeaways

Alright, let's wrap this up. We've covered a lot of ground, so let's recap the key points:

An Emergency Fund is Essential: If there's one thing I want you to take away from this chapter, it's this: an emergency fund isn't optional. It's a must-have. It's your financial safety net, there to catch you when life throws you a curveball. So, if you don't have one, start building it today. If you do have one, make sure it's adequate and keep it topped up.

Size Matters: When it comes to your emergency fund, size matters. Aim for 3-6 months' worth of essential living expenses. But remember, this is a guideline, not a rule. Your ideal emergency fund size depends on your personal situation. So, take the time to figure out what's right for you.

Use it Wisely: Your emergency fund is for emergencies. Not for holidays. Not for a new TV. Emergencies. So, use it wisely. And when you do use it, make sure to replenish it as soon as possible.

Review and Adjust: Your emergency fund isn't a set-it-and-forget-it thing. As your life changes, so should your emergency fund. So, review it regularly and adjust as needed.

In conclusion, building an emergency fund is one of the most important steps you can take towards financial freedom. It won't make you rich. It won't solve all your financial problems. But it will give you peace of mind. And that, my friend, is priceless. So, start building your emergency fund today. Your future self will thank you.

Chapter 15

Stay Motivated and Persistent

Embarking on a journey to become debt-free is not just a financial decision; it's a life-altering commitment. It's a testament to your determination, discipline, and willpower. This journey is a marathon, not a sprint, and it requires a level of tenacity and resilience that not everyone is prepared for. But you are. You've made the commendable decision to take control of your financial future, and for that, you should be proud.

In this chapter, we're going to delve deeper into the importance of staying motivated and persistent throughout your debt repayment journey. We're going to explore the role of motivation in debt repayment, the strategies you can use to maintain it, and how to stay laser-focused on your financial goals.

We'll also discuss how to navigate the inevitable setbacks and obstacles that you'll encounter along the way. These challenges are not roadblocks; they're stepping stones on your path to financial freedom. They're opportunities to learn, grow, and become stronger.

Moreover, we'll talk about the importance of incorporating wellness into your financial journey. Your financial health is deeply intertwined with your physical and mental health. Taking care of your overall well-being is not just good for you; it's good for your wallet too.

And let's not forget about the power of having a strong support system. Whether it's family, friends, financial advisors, or online communities, having people who support and understand your journey can make all the difference.

So, are you ready to dive in? Are you ready to explore the power of motivation, the importance of persistence, and the impact of wellness on your financial journey? Are you ready to learn how to stay focused, overcome obstacles, and build a strong support system?

Remember, the journey to debt freedom is not a straight line. It's a winding path with ups and downs, twists and turns. But with motivation, persistence, and the right strategies, you can navigate this path successfully. You can reach the peak of financial freedom and look out at the beautiful landscape of a debt-free life.

So, let's get started. Let's explore what it takes to stay motivated and persistent on your journey to debt freedom. Because you, my friend, have the power to change your financial future. And that journey starts right here, right now.

The Role of Motivation in Debt Repayment

Motivation is the fuel that drives the engine of success, especially when it comes to debt repayment. It's the spark that ignites the fire of action, the force that propels you forward even when the road gets tough. Understanding the role of motivation in debt repayment is crucial to your journey towards financial freedom.

When you're dealing with debt, it's easy to feel overwhelmed. The numbers may seem daunting, the journey ahead arduous. But that's where motivation steps in. It's the driving force that keeps you going, the inner voice that tells you to keep pushing, keep striving, and keep fighting. It's what gets you up in the morning, ready to face the day, ready to tackle your debt head-on.

Moreover, motivation is a powerful tool for maintaining your mental health during the debt repayment process. Dealing with debt can be stressful, even anxiety-inducing. It can weigh on your mind, casting a shadow over your daily life. But when you're motivated, when you have a clear goal in sight and the determination to reach it, that stress becomes manageable. It becomes a challenge to overcome, not a burden to bear.

Motivation also plays a crucial role in decision-making. It's what pushes you to make the tough choices, to cut back on unnecessary expenses, to prioritize your spending. It's what encourages you to stick to your budget, even when temptation strikes. It's what reminds you of why you started this journey in the first place.

But motivation isn't a constant. It ebbs and flows, waxes and wanes. There will be days when your motivation is high, when you feel invincible, ready to conquer the world. And there will be days when your motivation is low, when the weight of your debt feels too heavy to bear. And that's okay. It's normal. What's important is that you recognize these fluctuations and find ways to reignite your motivation when it starts to wane.

Remember, motivation is more than just a feeling. It's a mindset. It's a commitment to yourself and your financial future. It's the belief that you can and will overcome your debt. And with that motivation, with that belief, there's no obstacle you can't overcome, no goal you can't achieve.

So, harness the power of motivation and use it to fuel our journey towards debt freedom. Because with motivation on your side, there's nothing you can't achieve.

Maintaining Motivation: Strategies and Tips

Maintaining motivation throughout your debt repayment journey is not just beneficial, it's essential. It's the glue that holds your financial plan together, the compass that keeps you on course. But how do you keep that motivational fire burning, especially when faced with challenges or setbacks? Here are some strategies and tips:

Set Clear and Achievable Goals: Goals give you a target to aim for, a destination to reach. They provide a sense of direction and purpose. When setting your financial goals, make sure they are SMART - Specific, Measurable, Achievable, Relevant, and Time-bound. Having clear, achievable goals can boost your motivation and provide a sense of accomplishment as you tick them off one by one.

Visualize Your Progress: Seeing is believing. Visualizing your debt reduction can be a powerful motivator. Consider using a debt repayment chart or app to track your progress. Each time you make a payment, update your chart or app. Seeing the debt decrease can provide a sense of achievement and spur you on to keep going.

Immerse Yourself in Motivational Resources: Surround yourself with positivity and inspiration. This could include reading books about financial management, listening to podcasts, watching TED talks, or following financial influencers on social media. These resources can provide valuable insights, practical tips, and the motivation you need to stay on track.

Celebrate Small Wins: Don't wait until you're completely debt-free to celebrate. Recognize and celebrate small victories along the way. Each debt payment, no matter how small, is a step towards your financial freedom. Celebrating these small wins can boost your motivation and make the journey more enjoyable.

Stay Positive: Maintaining a positive attitude is crucial. There will be challenges and setbacks, but try to view them as learning opportunities rather than failures. A positive mindset can help you overcome obstacles and keep your motivation high.

Seek Support: Don't underestimate the power of a strong support system. This could be family, friends, a financial advisor, or an online community of people on a similar journey. They can provide encouragement, share their experiences, and offer advice. Knowing you're not alone can be a powerful motivator.

Practice Self-Care: Your mental and physical health are crucial to maintaining motivation. Make sure to take time for yourself, eat healthily, exercise regularly, and get enough sleep. When you feel good, you're more likely to stay motivated and focused on your goals.

Motivation is not a one-time thing. It's a continuous process. It's about finding what drives you, what inspires you, and harnessing that energy to fuel your journey towards debt freedom. So, keep these strategies in mind, stay motivated, and keep pushing forward. You've got this!

Staying Focused on Financial Goals

Staying focused on your financial goals is like keeping your eyes on the prize. It's about knowing where you're headed and not letting anything distract you from your path. It's about having a clear vision of what you want to achieve and relentlessly pursuing it. Here's how you can stay laser-focused on your financial goals:

Create a Vision Board: A vision board is a powerful tool that can help keep your financial goals at the forefront of your mind. It's a visual representation of your goals, dreams, and aspirations. You can include pictures, quotes, or anything else that represents what you want to achieve. Place your vision board somewhere you can see it every day as a constant reminder of your goals.

Keep a Financial Journal: Writing down your goals, progress, and thoughts can be a great way to stay focused. It allows you to reflect on your journey, celebrate your successes, and identify areas for improvement. Regularly reviewing your journal entries can provide valuable insights and keep your financial goals top of mind.

Regularly Review Your Goals: Goals are not set in stone. They can and should be reviewed and adjusted as needed. Regularly reviewing your goals allows you to track your progress, celebrate your achievements, and make necessary adjustments. It keeps your goals relevant and ensures they align with your current financial situation and future aspirations.

Break Down Your Goals: Large goals can seem daunting. Breaking them down into smaller, more manageable goals can make them seem less overwhelming and more achievable. Each small goal you achieve brings you one step closer to your larger goal, keeping you motivated and focused.

Stay Disciplined: Discipline is the bridge between goals and accomplishment. It's about making the right choices, even when it's hard. It's about prioritizing your financial goals over immediate gratification. Staying disciplined can help you stay focused and on track towards achieving your financial goals.

Practice Mindfulness: Mindfulness is about being present and fully engaged in the current moment. When it comes to your financial goals, practising mindfulness can help you make conscious decisions, avoid impulsive spending, and stay focused on your long-term goals.

Stay Positive and Patient: Achieving financial goals takes time. It's important to stay positive and patient throughout the journey. Remember, every step you take, no matter how small, brings you closer to your goals. Celebrate your progress and don't get disheartened by the pace.

Remember, staying focused on your financial goals is a continuous process. It requires commitment, discipline, and perseverance. But with the right strategies and mindset, you can stay focused, achieve your financial goals, and create the financial future you desire. Keep your eyes on the prize and keep moving forward.

Overcoming Setbacks and Obstacles

Setbacks, obstacles, failures - they're all part of the journey. They're the hurdles you have to jump, the mountains you have to climb. But here's the thing: They're not there to stop you; they're there to strengthen you. They're not barriers; they're benchmarks. They're not stumbling blocks; they're stepping stones.

When you face a setback, don't back down. Embrace it. Learn from it. Use it as fuel to push harder, to go further. And when you encounter failure, don't let it define you. See it as a learning opportunity and a chance to grow. I mentioned this in chapter one: failure is not failure unless you accept it as such. Reframe it, flip it on its head and turn it into something useful. It's not a dead-end; it's a detour. It's not a setback; it's a setup for a comeback.

And when the road throws you a curveball, don't panic. Have a contingency plan. Be prepared to pivot, to adjust, to keep moving forward. Surprises aren't shocks; they're shifts. They're not there to derail you; they're there to redirect you.

And amidst all this, stay focused on your goals. Distractions? They're not attractions; they're detractions. They're not there to entertain you; they're there to drain you. So, when you face a distraction, don't get side-tracked. Stay focused. Keep your eyes on the prize.

Do you know what got me through my greatest challenges? The other challenges! Each one taught me something new, made me stronger, more resilient. Each one was a stepping stone, leading me to where I am today.

Here's the truth: You'll never be without a challenge, whether you know it or not. The only way to be challenge-free is to do nothing, which is a challenge in itself unless you're six feet under already. So, embrace the challenges. They're not there to break you; they're there to make you.

I've given up so many times in my life on so many things I can't even count that far. I've hit rock bottom, picked myself up, only to fall back down again. But each time, I learned. Each time, I grew. I feel like I've paid my dues and learned my lessons. And you know what? It's made me who I am today. It's made me stronger, more resilient, more determined.

So, face your challenges head-on. Embrace them. Learn from them. And most importantly, overcome them. Because you, my friend, are stronger than any setback, bigger than any obstacle, and capable of achieving anything you set your mind to. Let's do this. Let's overcome. Let's conquer. Let's win!

Incorporating Wellness into Your Financial Journey

Wellness and finance are, in fact, two sides of the same coin. You can't have one without the other. Your overall wellness, including your physical and mental health, plays a significant role in your financial journey. It's the fuel that keeps you going, the foundation that keeps you standing.

When you're physically healthy, you're more energized, more focused, more capable. You're able to work harder, think clearer, and make better decisions. Regular exercise, a healthy diet, and adequate sleep are not luxuries; they're necessities. They're not just good for your body; they're good for your wallet.

I want to give some special attention to sleep. There is that myth going around that sleep is for losers and you have to work 18 hours a day if you want to achieve your dreams. I personally think that's a dangerous myth. Of course, you have to work hard and make sacrifices, otherwise, you won't get anywhere, but I think there's a limit to that.

Opinions are split here. Some high achievers only sleep the minimum necessary to keep them functioning like 4 hours a night. Others say sleep is power and swear by the benefits of sleeping 9 to 10 hours a night. I personally think that anything under six hours puts you in the danger zone. It's very important to give your body the time it needs to recover, to replace dead cells and clear the waste. Ten hours, however, sounds like a waste of time. So find your sweet spot and give your body what it needs.

And let's not forget about mental health. Dealing with debt can be stressful, overwhelming, even debilitating. But when you take care of your mental health, you're better equipped to handle the stress, to overcome overwhelm, and combat the debilitation. Mindfulness, meditation, and therapy are not indulgences; they're investments. They're not just good for your mind; they're good for your finances.

But wellness isn't just about the physical and mental. It's also about the emotional, the social, the spiritual. It's about maintaining healthy relationships, pursuing meaningful hobbies, and practising self-care. It's about finding balance, achieving fulfilment, and experiencing joy. Because at the end of the day, what's wealth without health? What's money without happiness? What's success without fulfilment?

So, incorporate wellness into your financial journey. Make it a priority, not an afterthought. Take care of your body, your mind, and your soul. Because when you're healthy in all aspects of life, you're not just better equipped to handle the financial journey; you're better equipped to enjoy the destination.

Remember, wellness and finance are two sides of the same coin. You can't have one without the other. So, take care of your health, take care of your wealth, and take care of yourself.

Building a Support System

Building a support system is like constructing a safety net. You do that by surrounding yourself with people who lift you up, not drag you down. By having a team of cheerleaders, advisors, and confidants who are there for you, through thick and thin.

You see, the journey to financial freedom isn't meant to be walked alone. It's a road filled with twists and turns, ups and downs, triumphs and trials. And having a strong support system can make all the difference. It can be the difference between falling and getting back up, between giving up and pushing forward, between failing and succeeding.

Your support system could include family, friends, financial advisors, or online communities. These are the people who encourage you when you're feeling down, celebrate with you when you're on top of the world, advise you when you're at a crossroads, and listen to you when you just need to vent.

Family and friends can provide emotional support, a listening ear, and a shoulder to lean on. They're there to celebrate your victories, big and small, and to pick you up when you stumble. They're your cheerleaders, your confidants, your rock.

Financial advisors, on the other hand, can provide professional guidance, expert advice, and objective insights. They're there to help you navigate the financial maze, make informed decisions, and stay on track towards your financial goals. They're your coaches, your mentors, your guides.

And then there are online communities; forums, social media groups, blogs. These are places where you can connect with others who are on the same journey, where you can share experiences, exchange ideas, and gain insights. They're your peers, your comrades, your tribe.

So, build your support system. Surround yourself with people who lift you up, who inspire you, and who believe in you. Because the journey to financial freedom isn't meant to be walked alone. It's meant to be shared, to be celebrated and enjoyed.

Remember, you're not alone in this journey. You have a team of cheerleaders, advisors, and confidants ready to support you. So, lean on them, learn from them, and grow with them because together, you're stronger. Together, you're unstoppable. Together, you can conquer anything.

The Power of Persistence

Persistence is the fuel that keeps the engine running, the fire that keeps the flame burning, and the force that keeps the wheel turning. It's the key to overcoming obstacles, to achieving goals, and to realizing your dreams. It's the difference between giving up and going on, between failure and success, between mediocrity and greatness.

You see, the journey to financial freedom isn't a sprint; it's a marathon. It's not about how fast you can run; it's about how long you can keep running. It's not about getting there in a flash; it's about getting there for sure. And that, my friend, requires persistence.

Persistence means staying the course, even when the going gets tough. It means keeping your eyes on the prize, even when the road is long and winding. It's pushing forward, even when the odds are stacked against you and, not just starting the race, but finishing it.

But here's the thing about persistence: it's not just about stubbornly sticking to a plan. It's about being flexible, adaptable, and resilient. It's about knowing when to push harder, when to change course, and when to take a break. It's about learning from failures, bouncing back from setbacks, and rising above challenges.

So, stay motivated, stay focused, and stay persistent. Use the discipline and habits you developed while paying off your debt to your advantage. Use the lessons you learned, the strength you gained, and the resilience you built to propel you forward. Use the support system you built, the wellness practices you incorporated, the goals you set to guide you on your journey.

And remember, this isn't just about money. It's about freedom. It's about living the life you want to live, without financial stress holding you back. You're creating a future that's not just debt-free, but abundant. You're going beyond just surviving, to truly thriving.

So, go out there and make it happen. You've got this. You've got the firepower, the potential, the persistence to change your financial future. And that, my friends, is the power of persistence.

Chapter 16

Going Beyond

So you got out of debt; now what? I'm going to tell you straight up; This is where the magic happens. You've done the hard work, you've clawed your way out of the financial pit, and now you're standing on the precipice of a whole new world. A world where you're not just surviving, but thriving. A world where you're not just debt-free, but financially free. And let me tell you, it's a beautiful place to be.

But before we break out the champagne and start celebrating, let's get one thing straight. This isn't the end of your journey. Oh no, far from it. This is just the beginning. You've conquered your debt, and that's a huge accomplishment. But now, it's time to set your sights on the next challenge. It's time to move beyond just being debt-free. It's time to start building wealth and creating abundance.

You see, being debt-free is like standing at base camp of Mount Everest. You've made it through the treacherous journey to get here, and you've got a great view. But you're not at the top yet. The real challenge, the real adventure, is just beginning. And let me tell you, the view from the top is worth every step.

So, are you ready? Are you ready to take the next step on your financial journey? Are you ready to move beyond debt and start building a life of financial freedom and abundance? I hope so because that's what this chapter is all about.

Financial Freedom

Financial freedom is a term that gets thrown around a lot, but what does it really mean? Well, let me paint you a picture. Imagine waking up in the morning and not having to worry about money. Imagine being able to do what you want, when you want, without having to think about whether you can afford it or not. Imagine having the freedom to make choices based on what makes you happy, not what makes your wallet happy. That, my friends, is financial freedom.

Financial freedom is more than just having money. It's having control over your finances and not letting them control you. It's being able to weather financial storms without panicking and having the freedom to make choices that allow you to enjoy life and provide for your future.

When you're financially free, you're not tied down by the chains of debt or living payslip to payslip. You have the freedom to invest, to grow your wealth, and to take advantage of opportunities that come your way. Want to start a business? Go for it. Want to invest in real estate? Nothing's stopping you. Want to take a year off and travel the world? Pack your bags and bon voyage!

But here's the thing about financial freedom. It doesn't just happen. It's not a lottery win or a stroke of luck. It's a journey. It's a series of choices and actions that lead you towards your goal. And the first step on that journey is understanding the opportunities that financial freedom opens up for you.

The Power of Momentum

Let's talk about momentum. You know, that thing that keeps you going when you're on a roll. That thing that makes it easier to keep moving forward once you've started. That thing that turns a small snowball into a massive avalanche. Yeah, that's momentum. And let me tell you, it's a powerful thing.

You've already experienced the power of momentum in your journey to becoming debt-free. You started by making small changes, maybe cutting back on expenses or paying off a small debt. And as you saw progress, you were motivated to do more. You gained momentum, and that momentum carried you forward, helping you to tackle bigger and bigger challenges until you were finally debt-free.

Now, here's the exciting part. That momentum you've built up? It doesn't have to stop just because you're debt-free. In fact, it can be the driving force that propels you towards financial freedom and wealth creation.

Think about it. You've already developed the discipline and habits necessary to manage your money effectively. You've learned how to budget, how to save, and how to make smart financial decisions. These skills, these habits, they're not just useful for getting out of debt. They're the foundation of wealth creation.

So, don't let that momentum go to waste. Leverage it. Use it to propel you forward on your journey to financial freedom. Use it to help you build wealth and create abundance. Because the same discipline and habits that got you out of debt can also make you rich. And that, my friends, is the power of momentum.

Multiple Streams of Income

Now, I know what you're thinking. "Multiple streams of income? I'm barely managing one!" But hold your horses. Having multiple streams of income doesn't mean you're working 80-hour weeks or juggling three jobs. It's about diversifying where your money comes from, so you're not reliant on a single source. It's about creating a financial safety net, so if one source of income dries up, you've got others to fall back on. It's about making money while you sleep. Sounds good, right?

Let's break down what these multiple streams of income could look like:

Your Day Job: This is probably your main source of income right now. It's reliable, it's steady, and it pays the bills. But it shouldn't be your only source of income. If the pandemic has taught us anything, it's that no job is 100% secure. So, don't put all your eggs in this one basket.

Side Hustle: This is where you can let your creativity and passion shine. Maybe you're a whizz at graphic design, or you make the best homemade candles in town. Whatever it is, find a way to monetize it. And who knows? Your side hustle could one day become your main hustle.

Investments: This is where you make your money work for you. Investing in stocks, bonds, or real estate can provide a steady stream of income. And no, you don't need to be a millionaire to invest. There are plenty of investment platforms out there that cater to all budgets. Just remember to do your research and understand the risks before diving in.

Rental Income: Got a spare room gathering dust? Or perhaps a holiday home that's empty half the year? Renting out property can provide a significant income stream. And with platforms like Airbnb, it's easier than ever to connect with potential renters.

Online Business: The internet has opened up a world of opportunities for creating income. From starting a blog or a YouTube channel to opening an online store, the possibilities are endless. And the best part? You can run an online business from anywhere in the world.

Royalties: If you're a creative type, you could earn royalties from writing a book, creating a piece of music, or even inventing a product. It might take some time to start earning, but once the royalties start rolling in, they can provide a passive income stream for years to come.

Now, I'm not saying you need to do all of these. But even just adding one or two additional streams of income can make a big difference to your financial health. The goal here isn't to work yourself to the bone. It's to create sources of income that can work for you, even when you're not working.

So, don't be content with just one source of income. Start exploring ways to create multiple streams of income. Because the more streams you have, the closer you'll be to achieving financial freedom. And remember, in the world of wealth creation, the only limit is your imagination. So, get out there and start creating those income streams!

Investing 101

Alright, let's dive into the world of investing. Now, I know what you're thinking. "Investing? Isn't that just for Wall Street tycoons and people with monocles?" Well, I'm here to tell you that's a load of rubbish. Investing is for everyone. Yes, even you.

And it's a crucial part of building wealth and achieving financial freedom.

So, what exactly is investing? At its core, investing is about putting your money to work for you. It's about buying assets (things like stocks, bonds, mutual funds, or real estate) that have the potential to increase in value over time. It's about making your money grow, instead of just letting it sit in a bank account losing value thanks to inflation.

Now, let's talk about the different types of investments. First up, we have stocks. When you buy a stock, you're buying a tiny piece of a company. If the company does well, the value of your stock goes up. If it doesn't, well, you get the picture.

Next, we have bonds. When you buy a bond, you're essentially lending money to a company or government. In return, they agree to pay you back with interest after a certain period of time.

Then there are mutual funds. These are like a basket of different investments. When you buy a share of a mutual fund, you're buying a small piece of all the investments in that fund. This can be a great way to diversify your portfolio without having to buy lots of individual stocks or bonds.

And let's not forget about real estate. Buying property can be a great investment, whether you're renting it out to generate income or hoping it will increase in value over time.

Now, investing isn't without risk. The value of investments can go down as well as up. But here's the thing. The potential rewards can be significant. And the risk can be managed through, you guessed it, diversification.

So, don't be scared of investing. Embrace it. Learn about it. Get your money working for you because if you want to build wealth and achieve financial freedom, investing isn't just an option. It's a necessity.

Entrepreneurship

I know it sounds like that thing that other people do but this isn't some mystical realm reserved for the chosen few. It's a gritty, exciting, roller-coaster ride that's open to anyone with a bit of grit, a dash of resilience, and a healthy dose of determination.

Entrepreneurship is about creating value from nothing. It's about spotting a gap in the market, a need that's not being met, or a problem that's crying out for a solution, and then stepping up and saying, "I'll fix that." It's about taking control of your financial future and creating wealth on your own terms.

Now, let's break down some of the key aspects of entrepreneurship:

Solving a Problem: The most successful businesses are built on simple, powerful ideas that solve real problems. So, start by looking at the world around you. What problems do you see? What frustrates you? What could be done better? These are all potential business ideas. For example, maybe you live in a town with a lot of tourists but no decent hotels. Boom, there's your business idea: open a boutique hotel that caters to tourists.

Monetizing a Passion: Another approach to entrepreneurship is turning your passion into a business. Do you love baking? Start a cake business. Are you a fitness fanatic? Open a personal training studio. Are you a whizz at social media? Start a digital marketing agency. The key here is to find something you love doing and then figure out a way to make money from it.

Franchising: If the idea of starting a business from scratch scares you, franchising could be a good option. You'll get to run your own business but with the support and structure of an established brand. It's like entrepreneurship with training wheels.

Online Business: The internet has opened up a world of opportunities for entrepreneurs. You could start an online store, create a blog or YouTube channel, offer freelance services, or launch a software start-up. The possibilities are endless, and the start-up costs can be surprisingly low.

Side Hustles: If you're not ready to dive headfirst into full-time entrepreneurship, a side hustle could be a good way to dip your toe in the water. This could be anything from selling handmade crafts on Etsy to tutoring students in your spare time to renting out your spare room on Airbnb.

Entrepreneurship isn't a get-rich-quick scheme. You'll end up working for the worst boss you've ever had; yourself. It's hard work. It's risky. But it's also one of the most rewarding and fulfilling paths you can take. So, if you're ready to take control of your financial future, entrepreneurship could be the path for you.

Real Estate Wealth

Alright, let's talk about real estate, the age-old path to wealth that your grandparents probably nagged you about at every family gathering. And you know what? They weren't wrong. Real estate is a tried-and-true method for building wealth, and it's not as out of reach as you might think.

Real estate investing involves purchasing properties with the intention of making a profit. This could be through rental income, the resale of the property after its value has increased, or both. It's a tangible, stable investment that can provide both immediate cash flow and long-term growth.

Let's break it down:

Rental Properties: This is the classic real estate investment. You buy a property, you rent it out, and you collect a monthly income. It's like having a money-printing machine in your basement. But with great power comes great responsibility. You'll be responsible for maintenance, dealing with tenants, and all the other joys of being a landlord. Or you can buy many of them and hire a property manager to deal with it all.

House Flipping: This is the real estate equivalent of a high-intensity interval workout. It's fast, it's intense, and it can be very profitable. The idea is to buy a property at a low price, renovate it, and then sell it for a profit. But beware; this isn't as easy as those TV shows make it look. It requires a good eye for potential, solid knowledge of property values, and the ability to manage a renovation project. So fill your library before you fill your portfolio.

Real Estate Investment Trusts (REITs): If the thought of unclogging tenants' toilets or managing a renovation project makes you break out in a cold sweat, REITs could be a good option. REITs are companies that own, operate or finance income-generating real estate. You can invest in a REIT just like you would invest in a company's stock. It's a way to get into real estate without getting your hands dirty.

Commercial Real Estate: If you're feeling adventurous, commercial real estate could be an option. This could be anything from office buildings to shopping centres to industrial properties. The potential profits can be huge, but so can the risks and the investment required.

Property Development: This is the big league of real estate investing. It involves buying land, building properties, and then selling or renting them. It's a high-risk, high-reward strategy that requires significant capital, expertise, and a strong stomach for risk.

So, real estate isn't a magic bullet. It requires research, planning, and a good dose of patience. But if done right, it can be a powerful wealth-building tool. So, if you're ready to take the plunge, start doing your research, crunching the numbers, and scouting for properties.

Financial Planning and Goal Setting

Let's get down to brass tacks. We've been talking about all these shiny ways to make money, but it's all just smoke and mirrors if you don't have a plan. Yes, my friend, I'm talking about the unsexy, often overlooked, but absolutely essential world of financial planning and goal setting.

Think of financial planning as the unsung hero of your financial success. It's not just about budgeting and saving, although those are important. It's about setting financial goals and then creating a roadmap to reach them. It's about understanding where you are now, where you want to be, and the steps you need to take to get there. It's about making your money work for you, instead of you working for your money.

First, you need to set clear financial goals. What do you want your financial future to look like? Maybe you want to retire early and sip cocktails on a beach. Maybe you want to buy a house, travel the world, or start your own business. Whatever your dreams are, they're the foundation of your financial plan. Be specific, be realistic, and write them down.

Next, you need to assess your current financial situation. This is your financial reality check. How much are you earning? How much are you spending? How much are you saving? It might be a bit uncomfortable, but it's necessary.

Once you've got a clear picture of where you are and where you want to be, it's time to create a budget. A budget is your financial roadmap. It helps you control your spending, save more, and work towards your financial goals. Remember, a budget isn't a prison sentence. It's a tool to help you make better financial decisions.

Now, based on your goals and your budget, you need to plan for savings and investments. Decide how much you want to save and invest each month. Remember, every little bit helps. Even small amounts can grow into a substantial nest egg over time.

Of course, your financial plan isn't set in stone. It's a living, breathing thing that should evolve with your life and your goals. So, make sure you regularly review your plan and make adjustments as needed.

And if all this sounds overwhelming, don't be afraid to get help. A financial advisor can provide expert advice and help you create a financial plan that's tailored to your needs and goals.

Financial planning isn't about making sacrifices. It's about making choices. It's about deciding what's important to you and making a plan to achieve it. So, get out there, set some goals, and start planning your financial future. Your dream life is waiting.

Summary and Key Takeaways

We've navigated the treacherous waters of debt and climbed the mountain of financial freedom, and now we're standing on the precipice, ready to soar into the world of wealth and abundance. But before we strap on our wings, let's take a moment to reflect on the journey so far.

Financial freedom, as we've discovered, isn't just about escaping the shackles of debt. It's about having the freedom to live life on your terms, and to make choices that align with your values and aspirations. It's about having the resources to pursue your dreams, not just scrape by.

We've also learned that the discipline and habits you've honed during your debt repayment journey are your secret weapons in the battle for wealth. You've shown that you can set goals, make a plan, and stick to it. Now it's time to deploy those skills in the service of wealth creation.

We've explored the concept of diversification and the importance of having multiple streams of income. Whether it's earned income from your day job, passive income from your investments, or portfolio income from your assets, each stream adds to your financial river, carrying you towards your financial goals.

We've dipped our toes into the world of investing, dispelling the myth that it's a game for the rich and privileged. Investing is for everyone who wants to grow their wealth. It's about understanding the basics, doing your research, and making informed decisions. And remember, there's no time like the present to start investing.

We've also looked at entrepreneurship as a path to wealth creation. It's not for the faint-hearted, but if you've got a burning idea and the passion to see it through, it could be your golden ticket.

Real estate, we've discovered, is more than just bricks and mortar. It's a powerful tool for wealth creation. Whether you're renting out properties, flipping houses, or investing in REITs, there's a strategy that can work for you.

And finally, we've learned that financial planning is the thread that weaves all these elements together. It's about setting goals, making a plan, and sticking to it. It's about making your money work for you, not the other way around.

So, there you have it. The road to wealth and abundance is paved with knowledge, discipline, and action. You've got the knowledge. You've got the discipline. Now, it's time to take action. Go out there and create the financial future you deserve. The only thing standing between you and your financial goals is action.

And that, my friends, is what's beyond.

Conclusion

As we reach the end of this enlightening journey, it's time to pause, reflect, and consolidate the wealth of knowledge we've gathered. We've traversed a vast landscape of financial wisdom, from understanding the intricate psychology behind debt to learning about the diverse strategies for tackling it. We've also been privileged to hear inspiring stories from real people who have successfully navigated their way out of debt, their experiences serving as a beacon of hope and a testament to the power of resilience.

The first step towards financial freedom, as we've learned, is a seismic shift in mindset. It's not just about crunching numbers or making budgets; it's about fostering a winner's mindset that permeates every aspect of your life. This mindset is the bedrock upon which your financial success is built. It involves setting clear, ambitious goals, believing in your ability to achieve them, being bold enough to seize opportunities, taking decisive action, learning from failure, surrounding yourself with positive influences, and continuously investing in personal development.

We delved deep into the psychology behind debt, understanding how it impacts our behaviour, decision-making, and overall well-being. We discovered that debt is not just a financial problem; it's a psychological challenge that requires a holistic approach to overcome. We also distinguished between good and bad debt and learned how to leverage the former to build wealth while avoiding the latter.

We discussed the importance of understanding credit scores and how they impact our financial lives. We learned how to assess our financial situation, create a budget, increase income, and reduce expenses. We also explored different debt repayment strategies, including the debt snowball and avalanche methods, and considered debt consolidation and refinancing options.

We learned how to handle interactions with debt collectors and the importance of building an emergency fund to avoid future debt. We also explored the journey from debt freedom to financial abundance, with real-life case studies and interviews providing practical examples and motivation.

The journey to becoming debt-free is not a walk in the park. It requires commitment, discipline, and a willingness to make significant changes in your life. But as we've seen from the stories in this book, it is possible. And the rewards, peace of mind, financial stability, and the freedom to live life on your terms, are well worth the effort.

I want to remind you that financial freedom is not a distant dream; it's a tangible goal that's within your reach. You now have the tools and knowledge you need to conquer your debt and achieve your financial goals. But knowledge alone is not enough. You must take action. Start today, no matter how small the step may seem. Every journey begins with a single step, and every step you take brings you closer to your goal.

You are not alone in this journey. There are resources available to help you, and there are people who have walked this path before you and succeeded. Use their stories as inspiration and motivation.

But probably the most important thing you should take away from this book is something that's close to my heart, and that's the concept of resilience in the face of temporary defeat. As you embark on this journey towards financial freedom, it's inevitable that you'll encounter setbacks. You might miss a payment, incur an unexpected expense, or find that your debt is reducing at a slower pace than you'd hoped. When this happens, it's easy to feel disheartened and consider giving up. But I want to assure you that these moments of temporary defeat are not a sign of failure; they're a natural part of the journey.

Remember, every setback is a setup for a comeback. It's in these challenging moments that we learn the most about ourselves and our capabilities. So, when you face a setback, don't view it as a dead-end. Instead, see it as a detour that's leading you to a new path, a path that's potentially filled with even greater opportunities. "Obstacles don't block the path; they are the path" Zen Proverb.

Focus on the progress you've made so far, no matter how small it might seem. Every pound you've paid off is a step closer to your goal. Set smaller, achievable goals along the way to keep you motivated and celebrate each victory, however minor it may seem. This journey is not a sprint; it's a marathon. And every step you take, no matter how small, is a step in the right direction.

Develop a resilient mindset. Practice mindfulness and self-compassion. When you're feeling overwhelmed, take a moment to breathe, to ground yourself in the present, and to remind yourself of your strength and determination. Reframe your failures as opportunities to learn and grow. Remember, it's not about how many times you fall, but how many times you get back up.

When you face a roadblock, don't be afraid to seek help. Reach out to a mentor, a financial advisor, or a supportive friend. Stay accountable to your goals and remember, it's okay to ask for help. We're all in this together.

And finally, remember to keep a sense of humour. This journey is tough, but it's also filled with moments of joy, growth, and self-discovery. So, laugh at the absurdities, celebrate the victories, and keep pushing forward. You're stronger than you think, and you're capable of achieving great things.

So, as we conclude this journey together, I want to leave you with this final thought: Don't fear temporary defeat. Embrace it. Learn from it. Grow from it. Because it's these moments of temporary defeat that will ultimately lead you to your greatest victories.

Thank you for joining me on this journey. I wish you all the best as you embark on your own path to financial freedom. Remember, the future is in your hands so make it a prosperous one.

Printed in Great Britain
by Amazon